DK EYEWITNESS TRAVEL

TOP 10
VIENNA

MICHAEL LEIDIG
IRENE ZOECH

Top 10 Vienna Highlights

The Top 10 of Everything

DK Penguin Random House

CONTENTS

Vienna
Area by Area

Streetsmart

Within each Top 10 list in this book, no hierarchy of quality or popularity is implied. All 10 are, in the editor's opinion, of roughly equal merit.

Front cover and spine Vienna at sunset, seen from the North Tower of Stephansdom
Back cover The magnificent Upper Belvedere reflected in a fountain
Title page Detail of the Secession Building

The information in this DK Eyewitness Top 10 Travel Guide is checked regularly. Every effort has been made to ensure that this book is as up-to-date as possible at the time of going to press. Some details, however, such as telephone numbers, opening hours, prices, gallery hanging arrangements and travel information, are liable to change. The publishers cannot accept responsibility for any consequences arising from the use of this book, nor for any material on third-party websites, and cannot guarantee that any website address in this book will be a suitable source of travel information. We value the views and suggestions of our readers very highly. Please write to: Publisher, DK Eyewitness Travel Guides, Dorling Kindersley, 80 Strand, London WC2R 0RL, Great Britain, or email travelguides@dk.com

Welcome to
Vienna

Bold, Baroque and achingly beautiful, Vienna's storied streets owe much to the extravagant creative splurges of Empress Maria Theresa and Emperor Franz Joseph during the time of the Austro-Hungarian Empire. From the Ringstrasse's opulent façades to the imperial grandeur of Schloss Schönbrunn, Vienna epitomizes decadence in all its glory. With Eyewitness Top 10 Vienna, it's yours to explore.

Vienna is home to the Gothic spires of **Stephansdom** and the Prater's iconic **Giant Ferris Wheel** as well as the world-famous Lipizzaner horses of the **Spanish Riding School**. An enviable array of galleries and museums rub shoulders with dozens of cultural venues that draw visitors from all over the world. Holding court in the midst of it all is the vast **Hofburg** palace: the imposing royal home of the Habsburg family for over six centuries, with its gilded decor, fascinating heritage and sumptuous art.

Contemporary museums and cutting-edge architecture bring a modern buzz to this historical city in a pleasing juxtaposition of old and new. The city and its shimmering ballrooms have long been synonymous with the super-charged Viennese Waltz. Yet in Vienna's idiosyncratic districts you'll find a beguiling mishmash of hip streets and faded grandeur together with the exotic oils, spices and food stalls of the famous **Naschmarkt**.

Whether you're coming for a weekend or a week, our Top 10 guide brings together the best of everything the city has to offer, from a rich pedigree in classical music to a funky vintage scene. The guide gives you tips throughout, from seeking out what's free to avoiding the crowds, plus eight easy-to-follow itineraries, designed to tie together a clutch of sights in a short space of time. Add inspiring photography and detailed maps, and you've got the essential pocket-sized travel companion. **Enjoy the book, and enjoy Vienna.**

Clockwise from top: **Façade of the Staatsoper, Johann Strauss Monument, patterned roof of Stephansdom, view of the Upper Belvedere, Ferris wheel in the Prater, interior of Café Central, exterior of the Majolika Haus**

Exploring Vienna

Few capital cities are as slow-paced and leisurely as Vienna so take a cue from its relaxed café lifestyle. Its compact centre, with its jaw-dropping high culture and dazzling Habsburg-era palaces, is walkable, and it has a wonderful maze of backstreets that twist and turn as much as the Danube itself.

Vienna's Spanish Riding School, with its Lipizzaner stallions, is world famous.

Two Days in Vienna

Day ❶
MORNING
Start at the imperial **Hofburg** palace (see pp16–21) with a coffee under gilded chandeliers at **Café Hofburg** (see p98). Delve into the lives of the Habsburg monarchs at the Sisi Museum before visiting the world-renowned **Spanish Riding School** (see pp20–21). Pass the **Albertina** museum (see p91), with its wideranging collections of art, before having a gourmet Austrian lunch at **Restaurant im Hotel Ambassador** (see p76).

AFTERNOON
Head to the **Staatsoper** (see pp36–7) for a fascinating backstage tour. Then to the **Hotel Sacher** (see p142) for a slice of Sachertorte (chocolate cake) at a table with a view of the street – it's a perfect people-watching spot.

Map labels: from Schwedenplatz (via tram 1); The Hofburg; Stephansdo...; Naturhistorisches Museum; Spanish Riding School; Restaurant im Hotel Ambassador; Schmetterlinghaus; Hotel Sach...; Haus Mus...; Albertina; Museums-Quartier; Kunsthistorisches Museum; Hundertwasserhaus (via U-Bahn); Staatsoper; Secession Building; Prater (via U-Bahn); Naschmarkt; Karlskirch...; Schloss Schönbrunn (via U-Bahn); 0 metres 500; 0 yards 500

Day ❷
MORNING
Climb the 137-m (450-ft) South Tower of the elaborately tiled **Stephansdom** (see pp12–15) for mesmerizing views of the city. Afterwards, grab a kerbside table at **Café Diglas** (see p98) on Fleischmarkt to enjoy an *Einspänner* (cream-topped coffee) and a bite to eat overlooking the crowds.

AFTERNOON
To sightsee in vintage style, hop aboard tram 1 at Schwedenplatz to trundle around the Ringstrasse boulevard. Spend the rest of the day at the **MuseumsQuartier** (see pp34–5) in Museumsplatz. As well as the wealth of museums to dip into, the courtyards host dance, film festivals, recitals and DJs in fine weather.

The Staatsoper, Vienna's State Opera House, has an elegant interior.

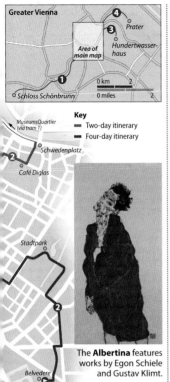

Stephansdom's brightly coloured patterned roof is instantly recognizable.

the fragrant gardens before a visit to the 6.5-ha (16-acre) **Stadtpark** *(see p62)* to see its beautiful sculptures.

AFTERNOON

At the **Albertina** *(see p91)* you'll find paintings, a million graphic works and thousands of early photographs. Enjoy a backstage tour at the **Staatsoper** *(see pp36–7)* before a visit to **Karlskirche** *(see pp32–3)*.

Day ❸

MORNING

After marvelling at the magnificent collections of the **Kunsthistorisches Museum** *(see pp22–5)*, delve into the artifacts at Vienna's two-storey **Naturhistorisches Museum** *(see p107)*.

AFTERNOON

Stop at the Leopold Museum in the **MuseumsQuartier** *(see pp34–5)* for the works of Gustav Klimt, and then head to the **Hundertwasserhaus** *(see pp40–41)*. The building's colourful façade has a real wow factor.

Day ❹

MORNING

Enjoy fun-filled family interaction at the **Haus der Musik** *(see p57)* before a visit to the **Schmetterlinghaus** *(see p69)*, home to hundreds of butterflies in a colourful tropical setting.

AFTERNOON

Pay a visit to the 1897 **Secession Building** *(see pp38–9)*, the former home of a breakaway group of artists led by Gustav Klimt. Round off the day exploring the **Prater** *(see p62)* – a former royal hunting ground – with its famous Ferris wheel.

The **Albertina** features works by Egon Schiele and Gustav Klimt.

Four Days in Vienna

Day ❶

MORNING

Browse **Stephansdom** *(see pp12–15)* before exploring the grandeur of the **Hofburg** palace *(see pp16–21)* and 450 years of tradition at the **Spanish Riding School** *(see pp20–21)*.

AFTERNOON

Meander through the exotic food stalls of the **Naschmarkt** *(see p116)*, piled high with produce. Next, head to **Schloss Schönbrunn** *(see pp42–5)*, the royal summer residence, for its Rococo rooms, fountains and gardens.

Day ❷

MORNING

Take time to stroll around the lovely **Belvedere** *(see pp28–31)* and admire

Top 10 Vienna Highlights

Detail of sculptural decoration on
the exterior of the Hofburg

🔟 Vienna Highlights

Splendid edifices, grand palaces and imposing churches that span the centuries make Vienna a wonderful city to visit, oozing both charm and atmosphere. Its imperial grandeur can still be felt, yet there's much more to offer, including stunning museums and a vibrant nightlife.

1 Stephansdom

The Gothic cathedral is one of the city's most prominent landmarks. From its spire you can enjoy spectacular views over the rooftops *(see pp12–15)*.

2 The Hofburg

The old imperial palace, with its many wings and courtyards and stunning interior, reflects Austria's glorious past. It is still the setting for grand balls *(see pp16–21)*.

Kunsthistorisches Museum 3

This remarkable museum contains one of the world's largest collections of Old Masters *(see pp22–5)*.

4 The Belvedere

The former summer residence of the 17th-century war hero Prince Eugene is a splendid Baroque palace that is now home to the Austrian Gallery. It houses Gustav Klimt's *The Kiss (see pp28–31)*.

5 Karlskirche
This impressive Baroque church has two columns on either side and a large dome overhead. It is a fine sight dominating Karlsplatz (see pp32–3).

6 MuseumsQuartier
The former imperial stables have been converted into a large museum complex exhibiting, among other things, collections of contemporary and modern art (see pp34–5).

7 Staatsoper
The Vienna State Opera attracts music lovers from all over the world. Its grand auditorium is a fitting introduction to an evening of classical music (see pp36–7).

8 Secession Building
The simple white Secession Building is a magnificent Art Nouveau edifice that reflects the ideals of the Secessionist movement – purity and functionalism (see pp38–9).

DER·ZEIT·IHRE·KVNST·
DER·KVNST·IHRE·FREIHEIT·

9 Hundertwasserhaus
Designed by Austrian artist Friedensreich Hundertwasser, this unconventional building is famous for its uneven floors, rooftop gardens and unique windows (see pp40–41).

10 Schloss Schönbrunn
The former summer home of the imperial Habsburg family remains a magnificent palace, with splendid Baroque gardens and the world's oldest zoo (see pp42–5).

⭐ Stephansdom

Located in the heart of the city, St Stephen's Cathedral is Vienna's most beloved landmark and Austria's finest Gothic edifice. The foundations of the original Romanesque church date back to 1147, but the earliest surviving features today are the 13th-century Giant's Door and the Heathen Towers on the west front. Various Habsburg rulers left their imprints by rebuilding the Gothic nave, the side chapels and the choir in the 14th and 15th centuries. The "Steffl", as the cathedral is called by the Viennese, suffered damage from World War II bombings, but its rebuilding was a symbol of hope as the country emerged from the ashes of the conflict.

3 Tiled Roof
The impressive roof is covered with almost 230,000 colourful tiles laid out in the form of the Habsburg coat of arms **(left)** – a double-headed eagle wearing the emperor's crown and the Golden Fleece. Originally built before 1474, the roof was restored after fire damage in World War II.

4 Giant's Door
After a mammoth's bone was found on the site during 15th-century construction works, the cathedral's main gate was renamed. It is decorated with sculptures that show Christ on Judgement Day between two angels.

1 Windows
The five medieval stained-glass windows behind the high altar relate biblical stories about the prophets and saints as well as the life and Passion of Jesus.

5 High Altar
Stephansdom's beautiful Baroque high altar **(above)** was created by the brothers Tobias and Johann Pock in 1647. The painting in the centre of the marble altar depicts the stoning of the cathedral's patron saint, St Stephen.

2 Organ
There has been an organ in the cathedral since 1334. The west choir organ **(above)**, with 125 stops and 10,000 pipes, was installed in the loft above the entrance in 1960.

6 Vaulting
The magnificent Gothic main nave of the cathedral is covered by an impressive ribbed vault supported by tall pillars.

7 North Tower with Pummerin

The North Tower, topped with a cupola, is home to the huge Pummerin bell. Weighing 21 tons, this great bell was cast from 100 cannon that were seized during the failed siege of Vienna by the Turks in 1683.

9 Catacombs

When Emperor Charles VI closed the cathedral cemetery in 1732, a catacomb system was built to bury the city's dead. By the end of the 18th century, about 11,000 people were laid to rest here. In the Duke's Crypt lie the remains of the Habsburg family.

10 West Front

The two imposing Romanesque Heathen Towers that flank the Giant's Door (above), and the two Gothic side chapels, with their filigree stone rose windows, are a spectacular welcome to the cathedral.

Stephansdom

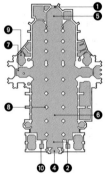

8 Pillars

The main nave of Stephansdom is dominated by soaring pillars, lavishly decorated with 77 clay and stone statues dating back to the 15th century.

NEED TO KNOW

MAP N3 ▪ Stephansplatz ▪ 01 515 52 3054 ▪ www. stephanskirche.at

Open 6am–10pm Mon–Sat, 7am–10pm Sun

Tours (English): 10:30am Mon–Sat; rooftop tour: Jul–Sep: 7pm daily

South Tower: stairs open 9am–5:30pm daily; adm €5

North Tower: lift open 8:15am–4:25pm daily; adm €6

Catacombs: open 10–11:30am & 1–4:30pm Mon–Sat, 1–4:30pm Sun & public hols; adm €6

▪ You can climb 343 steps to the top of the South Tower, or take a lift up the North Tower, for stunning views over the rooftops.

Cathedral Guide
Enter through the Giant's Door. The Gothic pulpit and North Tower lift are to your left. The catacombs' entrance is in the middle of the left side. In the far right corner is the raised tomb of Friedrich III (see p14).

Gothic Features in the Cathedral

1 Master Pilgram
A self-portrait of Master Anton Pilgram – one of the key craftsmen that worked on the cathedral – can be seen at the base of the old organ. He is holding his tools – a pair of compasses in his right hand and a set square in his left hand.

2 Fenstergucker
In this marvellous example of the Viennese late Gothic period, a sculpture of Master Pilgram himself leans out of an open window below the pulpit steps to inspect his work.

Stephansdom

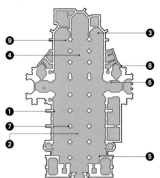

Fenstergucker below the pulpit

3 Raised Tomb of Friedrich III
Friedrich III commissioned Niklas Gerhaert van Leyden to create a majestic raised tomb for him. It took 45 years to build and was finished 20 years after the emperor's death. Little carved monks along the sarcophagus pray for his soul.

4 Baptismal Basin
Carved from red Salzburg marble, it took five years to finish this incredibly ornate 14-sided basin. Its decorations depict the seven holy sacraments, in the centre of which is Jesus's baptism.

5 Canopy with Pötscher Madonna
The 16th-century stone canopy shelters an icon of the Madonna from the Hungarian village of Máriapócs. In the 17th century the story spread that tears ran down Mary's cheeks and today people pray here for the sick to be healed.

6 Servants' Madonna
The graceful statue of the Madonna and Child is said to have miraculously helped acquit a maid who had been wrongly accused of stealing valuables from her master.

7 Pulpit
The lavishly decorated pulpit was created by Anton Pilgram in 1510. Lizards and toads, symbolizing evil, crawl up the balustrade, but they are fought off by a dog, the symbol of good.

Stephansdom's elaborate pulpit

JOHANNES CAPISTRANUS AND THE TURKISH SIEGE

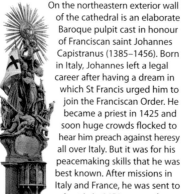

Johannes Capistranus' pulpit

On the northeastern exterior wall of the cathedral is an elaborate Baroque pulpit cast in honour of Franciscan saint Johannes Capistranus (1385–1456). Born in Italy, Johannes left a legal career after having a dream in which St Francis urged him to join the Franciscan Order. He became a priest in 1425 and soon huge crowds flocked to hear him preach against heresy all over Italy. But it was for his peacemaking skills that he was best known. After missions in Italy and France, he was sent to Austria in 1451 to preach against the Turkish invasion, and he led the Christian army to victory against the Turks in the battle of Belgrade in 1456. Johannes was canonized in 1724; the Austrians erected the pulpit in thanks later that century.

TOP 10
EVENTS IN THE CATHEDRAL'S HISTORY

1 The first church on the site is consecrated (1147)

2 St Stephen's gains the status of a diocese (1469)

3 Double wedding of Maximilian's grand-children to the children of the Hungarian king (1515)

4 Wolfgang Amadeus Mozart weds Constanze Weber (1782)

5 The catacombs are closed, due to an epidemic of the plague (1783)

6 Mozart's funeral (1791)

7 "October Revolution" rages in and around Stephansdom (1848)

8 Emperor Franz Joseph's funeral (1916)

9 Fire destroys the cathedral's roof (1945)

10 Funeral of Zita, wife of the last Austrian emperor, Charles I (1989)

The 1916 funeral procession of Emperor Franz Joseph I was filmed en route to the cathedral.

⑧ Cenotaph of Rudolph the Founder

Rudolph the Founder and his wife Katharina lie next to each other on their marble sarcophagus. The tomb was originally decorated with gold and precious jewels, and figures were placed in the little alcoves.

⑨ Wiener Neustädter Altar

The richly decorated altar just to the left of the main altar has four wings and shows 72 saints and scenes from the life of the Virgin Mary. Carved and painted in 1447, it was originally used as a shrine for relics.

Gargoyles at the top of the cathedral

⑩ Gargoyles

The gargoyles on the exterior roof of the cathedral are cast in the shape of dragons and other mythical animals in order to ward off evil.

TOP 10 ⭐ The Hofburg

The Hofburg, Vienna's former imperial palace, is a lavish complex of buildings spread over a large area within the city centre. Once home to emperors, the medieval castle was enlarged gradually up until 1918, and as the power of the Habsburgs grew, successive emperors added buildings – the Neue Burg (New Palace) is the most recent and grand section. Today the Hofburg houses the offices of the Austrian president, a convention centre, museums, state rooms and the Winter Riding School where the elegant white Lipizzaner stallions of the Spanish Riding School perform.

1 Swiss Gate
The name of this Renaissance gate **(above)** refers to the Swiss guards that were employed by Empress Maria Theresa in the 18th century.

NEED TO KNOW

MAP L4 ■ Innerer Burghof/ Kaisertor ■ 01 533 75 70 ■ www. hofburg-wien.at

Open Sep–Jun: 9am–5:30pm daily; Jul & Aug: 9am–6pm daily

Adm €13.90

■ Every Sunday the Vienna Boys' Choir sings at 9:15am in the Imperial Chapel. Book tickets in advance.

2 Austrian National Library
The Baroque library **(above)** was built by Josef Emanuel Fischer von Erlach from 1723 to 1726. It has priceless historic manuscripts in walnut bookcases.

3 Imperial Silver Collection
The elaborate serving bowl, table decorations and silverware in this collection show the splendour that marked meals at the imperial court.

The Hofburg

6 Heroes' Square

Equestrian statues of Prince Eugene of Savoy and Archduke Charles dominate Heldenplatz (Heroes' Square), formerly a parade ground **(left)**.

7 Secular and Ecclesiastical Treasuries

Magnificent artifacts are on display in 16 rooms dedicated to the relics of the Austrian and Holy Roman empires.

BUILDING THE PALACE

Every emperor left his mark on the palace until 1918. The Stallburg was built in the Renaissance under Maximilian II, while Amalienburg, constructed for his son Rudolph II, was completed in 1605. The oldest surviving part is the Schweizertrakt, featuring the Imperial Chapel and the Swiss Gate (1552–3).

8 Burggarten and Volksgarten

Both of these pretty parks owe their origins to the Napoleonic troops who blew up parts of the palace in 1809, creating open spaces **(above)**.

9 Imperial Chapel

Although the original interior with carved statuary was altered by Maria Theresa, the Burgkapelle (Royal Chapel) remains one of the oldest parts of the palace. Musicians including Mozart gave recitals here.

10 Imperial Apartments

The Kaiserappartements (private apartments) in the Amalia Wing are preserved as they were in the day of Franz Joseph and his wife Elisabeth *(see p19)*. Six rooms are dedicated to her as the Sisi Museum **(below)**.

4 Museums

The semicircular Neue Burg, with its vast colonnaded façade, is home to collections of musical instruments, arms and armour, and the Weltmuseum Wien ethnological museum.

5 Michaeler Gate

The large, majestic Michaeler Gate is the main entrance into the complex, and its imposing green dome with golden decorations looms over Michaelerplatz.

Artistic Treasures in the Hofburg

1 Crown of the Holy Roman Empire

Among the palace's exquisite collection of ecclesiastical and secular precious objects is this stunning gold crown, crafted in around AD 962 and decorated with cloisonné enamel and gemstones.

Bejewelled gold crown

2 Silverware and Porcelain

The *Silberkammer* displays the silverware and Augarten porcelain that was used for imperial banquets.

3 Austrian Sceptre and Orb

The enthroning of a new Habsburg ruler was accompanied by a ceremony of homage, during which the sovereign carried the sceptre and orb.

4 The Golden Fleece

This splendid chainmail armour, made in 1517, consists of a neck chain and a closed collar of double-walled plates.

5 Austrian National Library Frescoes

Daniel Gran painted these beautiful wall frescoes in the main hall in 1730 in honour of Emperor Charles VI. The statue in the middle of the room represents the emperor as the centre of the universe, holding a balance between war and peace.

6 Captain Cook Artifacts

Among the exhibits in the Weltmuseum Wien ethnological museum are artifacts acquired by British explorer Captain James Cook on his voyages around the globe, including masks from North America.

Ornate Cradle of the King of Rome

7 Cradle of the King of Rome

This cradle was given by Maria Louisa, Archduchess of Austria and second wife of Napoleon, to her son, the King of Rome. It is adorned with precious materials such as gold, silver and mother-of-pearl, while a goddess of victory crowns the child with a diadem of stars and a laurel wreath (**above**).

8 Aztec Feather Headpiece

The Penacho is the only one of its kind in existence today. Restoration of the 450 green-tail Quetzal feathers and 1,000 gold plates was a joint project with Mexico.

National Library

9 **Portrait of Empress Elisabeth**

German painter and renowned court portraitist Franz Xavier Winterhalter painted this famous portrait of the Empress Elisabeth in 1865. It hangs in one of the rooms of the Sisi Museum *(see p17)*.

10 **Historic Globes**

This collection *(see p67)* unites more than 300 globes and astrological instruments, including two globes by Venetian cartographer Vincenzo Coronelli made for Emperor Leopold I at the end of the 17th century.

Historic globes collection

FRANZ JOSEPH AND SISI

Born in 1830, Franz Joseph was crowned Emperor of Austria in 1848, aged 18. He met his wife, Princess Elisabeth of Bavaria, lovingly known to Austrians as "Sisi", in 1853 and they married shortly after. The empress was adored by Austrians, then as now, for her extraordinary beauty, dignity and elegance in state matters. Many believed Franz Joseph's social successes were the result of Sisi's influence, and they considered her their "real" sovereign. The lives of the emperor and empress were not without trials and sorrows, however. Franz Joseph lost major wars to France (1848) and Prussia (1866), despite being crowned King of Hungary in 1867. They also suffered many personal

Empress Elisabeth

tragedies – the emperor's brother, Maximilian, was executed in Mexico and his only son, Crown Prince Rudolph, committed suicide in 1889, after which Sisi dressed only in black. Austria, too, fell into mourning in 1898 when their beloved empress was assassinated in Geneva. Franz Joseph ruled for 68 years, until his death in 1916.

TOP 10 EVENTS IN THE HOFBURG

1 A fort is built on the site of today's Hofburg (1275)

2 The Alte Burg wing is built under Ferdinand I (1547–52)

3 Fischer von Erlach starts building the Winter Riding School (1729)

4 Carousels with the Lipizzaner horses are staged in the Winter Riding School (1740–80)

5 Mozart gives musical performances regularly in the Burgkapelle between 1781 and 1791

6 The Vienna Congress is held (1815)

7 The Michaeler wing is built (1889–93)

8 World War I prevents the construction of the second wing (1918)

9 Hitler proclaims the annexation of Austria to the Third Reich from the balcony of Neue Burg (1938)

10 Fire destroys the ballroom in the Redoute wing (1992)

Spanish Riding School

Spanish Riding School horses and riders at the Winter Riding School

1 Horses' Steps

The steps of the famous white Lipizzaner stallions of the Spanish Riding School follow the rigid patterns of the "high art" of riding which was established during the Renaissance period. Agility and strength are the goals. The most difficult part of the performance is the quadrille, which involves a precise and exact framework of choreography.

2 Emperor's Box

Once reserved for the imperial family, the royal box still has the best seats in the house.

Riders in the Emperor's box

3 Portrait of Charles VI

A portrait of Charles VI riding on a white stallion hangs in the royal box. Riders entering the hall pay respect to the founder of the school by raising their bicorn hats to the painting.

4 Lipizzaner Horses

The elegant white Lipizzaner stallions are bred at the national stud farm at Piber. The foals are born dark-skinned or black and acquire their trademark white coat between the ages of four and ten.

Lipizzaner horse and rider

5 Training

The horses move from the stud farm to the Spanish Riding School when they are about four years old and are then trained for a minimum of eight years, or until they are skilled enough to perform.

6 Riders

Just like the horses, the riders at the school have to go through an extensive training period before they can perform classical dressage and other riding techniques. The riders traditionally wear white jodhpurs and a double-breasted coffee-brown coat with brass buttons.

7 Stables
This Renaissance building in the Stallburg section of the Hofburg has an impressive three-storey gallery. It was built during the reign of Emperor Maximilian II.

8 Winter Riding School
Since 1735 the Spanish Riding School has been located in the Winter Riding School building, designed by Fischer von Erlach in Baroque style.

9 Interior
The horses perform their elegant ballet in the 56-m- (180-ft-) long hall. The gallery here is supported by 46 Corinthian columns.

10 Summer Riding School
During the summertime, performances and training sessions at the Spanish Riding School are carried out in a courtyard adjoining the Winter Riding School.

THE HISTORY OF THE LIPIZZANER HORSES

Spanish horses were first brought to Austria from Spain by Emperor Maximilian II in 1562, and the first evidence of them being housed in the Spanish Riding School dates back to 1572. In 1580, the horses were given the name Lipizzaner after a stud farm in Trieste; around the same time the first riding hall was built at the present location. The school we know today was formed in the 19th century and hosted equestrian events where the horses performed in graceful formations. For 436 years, riders were exclusively male. In 2008, two women, one Austrian and one British, were accepted into the school. Riding costumes have remained unchanged from the "Empire Style" of 1795.

TOP 10 PIECES OF TACK AND DRESS

1 Bicorn Napoleon hats
2 Brown cut-away tailcoats
3 Buckskin breeches
4 Knee-high black boots
5 Swan neck spurs
6 Buckskin saddle
7 Pale suede gloves
8 Gold-plated bridles
9 Saddlecloth colour indicates status of rider
10 Gold-plated horse breastplate

This late 19th-century painting, *Morning Training in the Winter Riding School* (1890) by Italian painter Julius von Blaas, shows several of the graceful stallions practising their exercises in the elegant surroundings of the riding school.

🔟 ⭐ Kunsthistorisches Museum

Built in Italian Renaissance style by architects Karl von Hasenauer and Gottfried Semper, the impressive Kunsthistorisches Museum was opened in 1891. The majestic architecture creates a fitting setting for the artistic treasures assembled by the Habsburgs, who were enthusiastic patrons and collectors for centuries. The museum's collections, particularly the Old Masters, are among the most important and spectacular found anywhere in the world.

1 Large Self-Portrait

The Dutch master artist Rembrandt painted this canvas in 1652, depicting everything around him in dark colours, with his face the only area of light.

2 Peasant Wedding

More than any of his other works, this 1568 painting contributed to Pieter Brueghel the Elder's fame as a portrayer of peasant life. The viewer feels right in the middle of a rustic wedding (**below**).

3 Blue Hippo

Hippo figurines are often found in the tombs of Ancient Egypt, as they were thought to help gain entry into the afterlife. This one has drawings of plants from the Nile Delta on its body (*see p24*).

4 Virgin and Child with a Pear

German artist Albrecht Dürer (1471–1528) painted many Madonna pictures, but this one is among the best known (**left**). It shows the Virgin Mary bending over a child holding a pear core.

5 The Fur

This 1638 painting is the most intimate portrait of Peter Paul Rubens' wife Hélène, whom he married late in life and whose features he often incorporated into his works (**above**). In a naturally graceful pose, the young woman evokes Venus, goddess of love.

6 Maria Theresa's Breakfast Service

Crafted in Vienna around 1750, this pure gold set belonged to the empress and consists of about 70 pieces, including a stunning gold teapot. Some items, such as a mirror and a basin, are part of a washing set.

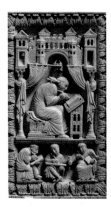

7 St Gregory with the Scribes

This late-9th-century ivory carving from Germany (left) shows St Gregory and three scribes.

8 Madonna of the Cherries

A number of paintings by Titian can be found in the Italian Collection. In this one (1518), the Madonna's dress is painted in the red-brown colours for which the artist is known.

9 Summer

From 1562, Italian Giuseppe Arcimboldo served as portrait artist at the court of Rudolph II. He became famous for his heads composed of fruits and vegetables which served as allegorical representations (below).

Kunsthistorisches Museum

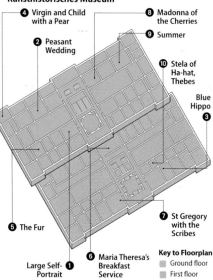

- 4 Virgin and Child with a Pear
- 2 Peasant Wedding
- 8 Madonna of the Cherries
- 9 Summer
- 10 Stela of Ha-hat, Thebes
- Blue Hippo 3
- 5 The Fur
- 7 St Gregory with the Scribes
- 1 Large Self-Portrait
- 6 Maria Theresa's Breakfast Service

Key to Floorplan
- ▨ Ground floor
- ▨ First floor

10 Stela of Ha-hat, Thebes

The stela (stone slab), which is more than 2,500 years old, is lavishly painted in gold, red and blue and depicts Osiris among other Egyptian gods, who are praised in the inscriptions. The stela was discovered inside a tomb in Thebes.

NEED TO KNOW

MAP K5 ■ Maria-Theresien-Platz ■ 01 525 240 ■ www.khm.at

Open Jun–Aug: 10am–6pm daily (until 9pm Thu); Sep–May: 10am–6pm Tue–Sun (until 9pm Thu)

Adm €15 (free entry for under 19s)

Audio guides available

■ Don't forget to admire the stunning view of the white marble floor with black patterns from the café on the first floor.

Museum Guide

The main entrance is on Maria-Theresien-Platz. As you enter, collect a map to guide you. On the ground floor are the Egyptian Collection and the Greek and Roman Antiquities to your right, while the left wing hosts the magnificent Kunstkammer (Chamber of Art and Wonders). The staircase takes you to the Picture Gallery where the most famous paintings are located. The Coin Cabinet and Vermeyen cartoons are on the second floor.

The Kunsthistorisches Collections

1 The Vermeyen Cartoons

These large cartoons, or sketches, depict various scenes from Emperor Charles V's Tunis campaign of 1535. They were produced by court painter Jan Cornelisz Vermeyen (who accompanied the emperor on the campaign). Willem de Pannemaker used them as models for 12 tapestries that now hang in Madrid.

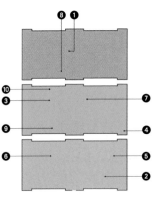

Key to Floorplan   **Kunsthistorisches**
⬜ Ground floor   **Museum**
⬜ First floor
⬛ Second floor

Detail from a Vermeyen cartoon

2 Egyptian Collection

This section has a remarkably extensive stock of pieces from the Old and Middle Kingdoms of Ancient Egypt. The collection was amassed in the 19th and 20th centuries, developed by purchases, donations and new acquisitions from excavations.

Ancient Egyptian blue hippo

3 Flemish Collection

A great number of works from 17th-century Flanders made their way into the museum because of Habsburg family ties to this part of Europe. The highlights are works by Rubens and Jan van Eyck.

4 Spanish and French Collection

Thanks to Habsburg family ties, portraits of the Spanish royal family form part of the collection. Diego Velázquez's portraits of the Infanta Margarita Teresa (daughter of Philip IV) are on display.

5 Greek and Roman Antiquities

The collection, originating from the former estate of the Habsburgs, covers a period of history extending from 3rd-century-BC Cypriot Bronze Age pottery to Slavic finds from the beginning of the 1st century AD.

It is also internationally renowned as the home of the unique cameos and archaeological treasures dating from the Great Migration and the Early Middle Ages.

6 Kunstkammer (Chamber of Art and Wonders)

Completely redesigned in 2013, this magnificent collection was amassed by emperors and aristocrats in the Renaissance and Baroque periods. The Kunstkammer has 20 galleries and 2,200 pieces, and is justifiably known as "a museum within a museum". Natural objects to which were ascribed magical powers vie with masterpieces such as Maria Theresa's breakfast service and the celebrated *Saliera* (salt cellar) by Benvenuto Cellini *(see p22)*.

7 Italian Collection

The majority of the 15th- to 18th-century Italian paintings were collected by Archduke Leopold Wilhelm, who founded the collection in the 17th century. They are mainly from the Venetian Renaissance, with major works by Titian, Veronese, Canaletto and Tintoretto.

8 Coin Cabinet

More than 700,000 coins, medals and banknotes from three millennia are on display in this fascinating numismatic collection.

Holbein's portrait of Jane Seymour

9 German Collection

The German collection has many 16th-century paintings. Among them are works by Dürer, Cranach the Elder and Holbein the Younger.

Coin Cabinet exhibit

10 Dutch Collection

This section (15th to 17th century) includes a large collection of works by Pieter Brueghel the Elder, containing about a third of all his surviving pictures.

Crucifixion Triptych (c.1445) by Rogier van der Weyden in the Dutch Collection

Following pages Naiad Fountain at Schloss Schönbrunn

TOP 10 ⭐ The Belvedere

Prince Eugene of Savoy, the most celebrated of the Habsburg generals owing to his defeat of the Turks in 1683, commissioned the two Belvedere palaces (Upper and Lower) with the money he received as a reward for his victories during the Spanish Succession. The payment allowed him to carry out one of the most ambitious building projects ever undertaken by a private individual. The palaces were built by Lukas von Hildebrandt in 1714–23 as the prince's summer residence and are a shining example of Baroque style.

1 Upper Belvedere
Built to impress, and never inhabited, this elaborate palace (above) houses the greatest collection of Austrian art in the world, dating from medieval times to today.

2 Marble Hall
The most beautiful room within the Upper Belvedere, this has a lavish frescoed ceiling (below). The Austrian State Treaty was signed here in 1955.

3 Sala Terrena
Set on the ground floor, beneath the Marble Hall, is the beautiful Sala Terrena hall, with four massive statues supporting the vaulted ceiling. White stuccowork covers the walls and ceiling.

4 Lower Belvedere
The opulent Baroque palace, set in beautiful landscaped gardens, was the former living quarters and state rooms of Prince Eugene. It now houses special exhibitions only.

5 Marble Gallery
Constructed with niches to hold classical statues, this grandiose room has a stucco ceiling showing a heroic Prince Eugene being honoured.

6 Orangery and Palace Stables
Adjacent to the Lower Belvedere, the Orangery is a modern white exhibition space. The Stables feature examples of different painting styles.

8 Gold Cabinet
A statue of Prince Eugene of Savoy stands in this Lower Belvedere room **(above)**. The walls are entirely covered by huge gilt-framed mirrors.

9 21er Haus
This Modernist building was Austria's pavilion for Expo 58 (Brussels' World Fair in 1958). It was moved to Vienna and is now a museum of contemporary art. It also has an interesting cinema and workshop programme.

7 French Gardens
The Baroque gardens and terraces include the private flowers of Prince Eugene and Europe's oldest alpine gardens.

10 Garden Statues
Of the numerous statues dotted around the gardens, the Eight Muses and the Sphinxes **(right)** are the most outstanding.

The Belvedere

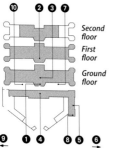

Second floor
First floor
Ground floor

Key to Floorplan
■ Upper Belvedere
■ Lower Belvedere

NEED TO KNOW

Upper Belvedere: MAP G6; Prinz-Eugen-Strasse 27; 01 795 57 134; 9am–6pm daily (until 9pm Fri); adm €15; www.belvedere.at

Lower Belvedere, Orangery, Palace Stables: MAP F5; Rennweg 6; 01 795 57 134; 10am–6pm daily (until 9pm Fri), Palace Stables: 10am–noon daily; adm €13; www.belvedere.at

21er Haus: MAP H6; Quartier Belvedere, Arsenalstrasse 1; 01 795 57 134; open 11am–6pm Wed–Sun (until 9pm Wed & Fri); adm €8; www.belvedere.at

■ A range of combined tickets, all valid for up to 30 days, is available for various combinations of Belvedere venues. Entry for under-19s is free. See the website for details.

Artworks in the Belvedere

1 Napoleon at the Saint Bernard Pass

Jacques-Louis David's idealized rendering of Napoleon (1803) depicts him crossing the Alps into Italy in 1801 on a white stallion. In fact, Bonaparte made this journey on a mule.

2 Still Life with Dead Lamb

Seen as a metaphor of a world that has lost its way, this still life (1910) is one of the most important works by Oskar Kokoschka.

3 Cliff Landscape in the Elbe Sandstone Mountains

German Romanticist Caspar David Friedrich sought to contrast the artifice of human civilization with natural landscapes, which he saw as the sublime product of divine creation. In this landscape (1822–3), the tree stumps remind viewers of their transience, while the mountain peaks symbolize God's constant presence.

4 Character Heads

Franz Xavier Messerschmidt was one of the most eccentric artists of the 18th century. His "Character Heads" (1770–83) series presents busts with extreme facial expressions. Among the highlights is the amusing *Intentional Jester.*

The Belvedere

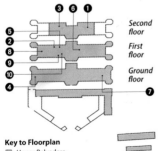

Second floor

First floor

Ground floor

Key to Floorplan
◼ Upper Belvedere
◼ Lower Belvedere

Gerstl's *Self-Portrait, Laughing*

5 Self-Portrait, Laughing

Painted the same year that he committed suicide (1908), Richard Gerstl tries a last attempt at defiant self-definition.

6 The Chef

Claude Monet painted only a few portraits. This 1882 work (also known as *Le Père Paul*) shows the renowned chef Paul Antoine Graff, who owned a small hotel on the Normandy coast at which Monet stayed. Monet's depiction of the 60-year-old wearing a chef's hat and whites captures his facial expression with skilful spontaneity.

7 Znaimer Altarpiece

The carved inner sides of this magnificent triptych (c.1427) depict the events of Good Friday as recorded in the Gospel of St Matthew. The story is supplemented by scenes taken from the Apocrypha.

8 The Kiss

Painted in 1909, Gustav Klimt's most celebrated work, *The Kiss*, features the linear style and organic forms that would characterize the work of the Secessionists.

9 Death and the Maiden

A man and a woman are clutching each other on a sheet spread over uneven terrain in this painting (1915). Artist Egon Schiele painted his own features on the man.

10 Farmhouse in Upper Austria

Although Klimt is largely known for his figure paintings, landscapes also played a key part in his work. From 1900 he spent most summers in the Salzkammergut, painting scenes such as this (1911).

Klimt's *Farmhouse in Upper Austria*

THE SECESSIONIST MOVEMENT

Formed in 1897, the Secessionist style was a reaction against the conservative "historicism" of the Association of Austrian Artists, Vienna's dominant artistic union, which still flourishes and today occupies the Künstlerhaus *(see p59)*. The leader and first president of the breakaway Union of Austrian Artists was Gustav Klimt. Founding members included Koloman Moser, Josef Hoffmann, Max Kurzweil and Wilhelm Bernatzik. Architect Otto Wagner joined later. The group was called the "Vienna Secession", as their movement followed similar rebellions in Berlin and Munich. Secessionism has no single defining stylistic theme, aside from the desire to eliminate historical influences. Their masterpiece is the Secession Building *(see p38)*.

TOP 10 AUSTRIAN 19TH- AND 20TH-CENTURY ARTISTS

1 Gustav Klimt (1862–1918)

2 Kolo Moser (1868–1918)

3 Richard Gerstl (1883–1908)

4 Oskar Kokoschka (1886–1980)

5 Egon Schiele (1890–1918)

6 Maria Lassnig (1919–2014)

7 Friedensreich Hundertwasser (1928–2000)

8 Hermann Nitsch (b.1938)

9 Christian Ludwig Attersee (b.1940)

10 Arnulf Rainer (b.1948)

Having visited Ravenna and Venice in Italy, Klimt was inspired by the gilded mosaics he saw there and adapted the idea into his glittering, erotic work *The Kiss*.

TOP 10 ⭐ **Karlskirche**

St Charles' Church was built between 1715 and 1737 to honour Karl Borromeo, patron saint of the fight against the plague. The aim was to thank God for delivering Vienna from the plague epidemic in 1713 that had claimed more than 8,000 lives. Emperor Charles held a competition among architects to design the church, which was won by Johann Fischer von Erlach. The Baroque masterpiece has a dome and portico borrowed from Classical architecture, while there are Oriental echoes in the minaret-like columns.

④ **Cupola with Frescoes**

The fresco by Johann Michael Rottmayr on the interior of the dome depicts the Virgin Mary begging the Holy Trinity to deliver the population from the plague.

① **Altar Paintings**

The side altars boast several paintings, but the most remarkable are those by master artist Daniel Gran **(above)**. His famous paintings *The Healing of a Gout Victim*, *Jesus and the Roman Captain* and *Saint Elisabeth of Hungary* can be found in the church.

⑤ **Pediment Reliefs**

The pediment resembles the covering of a Greek temple. Its reliefs, designed by Giovanni Stanetti, show the suffering of the Viennese during the 1713 plague.

② **Karl Borromeo Statue**

Designed by Lorenzo Mattielli, this statue of the patron saint of the fight against the plague sits on the church's pediment.

③ **Entrance**

The stunning façade is winged by two gatehouses that are reminiscent of Chinese pavilions and lead into the side entrances. At the centre of the façade is the stairway, at the top of which is a Classical pediment supported by six pillars **(below)**.

⑥ **Columns**

Inspired by the ancient Roman column of Trajan, the church's two huge columns are decorated with scenes from the life of St Karl Borromeo. The left column shows the quality of steadfastness, while the column on the right shows courage.

NEED TO KNOW

MAP F4 ▪ 01 505 62 94 ▪ Karlsplatz ▪ www.karlskirche.at

Open 9am–6pm Mon–Sat; noon–7pm Sun & holidays

Adm €8 (including lift)

▪ Take the lift to the top of the dome to get a look at the frescoes on its interior and to enjoy the amazing city views.

JOHANN FISCHER VON ERLACH

Many of Vienna's finest buildings were designed by Johann Fischer von Erlach (1656–1723). The Graz-born architect studied in Rome, and then moved to Vienna, where he became the court architect and a leading exponent of the Baroque style. He designed a great many churches and palaces, notably Karlskirche and the university church at Salzburg. Moreover, he sketched the initial plans for Schönbrunn Palace (see pp42–5). After Erlach's death in Vienna, Karlskirche was completed by his son.

9 Pulpit
The church's richly gilded pulpit is surmounted by two cherubs on the canopy and is decorated with *rocailles* (scrolls) and garlands of flowers.

7 High Altar
The high altar **(above)**, designed in typical Baroque style, was probably planned by Fischer von Erlach himself. It features a stucco relief by Albert Camesina showing St Karl Borromeo being taken into heaven on a cloud laden with angels and cherubs.

8 Pond with Henry Moore Sculpture
The church's setting is as impressive as its interior. In front of the church is a stone-paved pond with a modern Henry Moore sculpture in the centre, which is deliberately intended to contrast with the ornate Baroque style of the church.

10 Angels
Two angels guard the exterior stairway. The angel on the left represents the Old Testament; the one on the right, the New Testament **(below)**.

Karlskirche

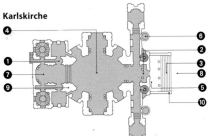

TOP 10 ⭐ MuseumsQuartier

Today one of Europe's most vibrant cultural complexes, the Museum Quarter's first buildings, some 300 years ago, were stables, home to the emperor's horses. They were commissioned by Charles VI in 1713 and completed by Johann Fischer von Erlach in 1725, with the stables being transformed into an exhibition ground in 1918. The MQ, as it is called, now houses more than 70 cultural centres, in varying styles, with shops and restaurants. In summer, the main courtyard is filled all day and night. Underground parking, free Wi-Fi and a maze of passageways opening into seven art-filled courtyards attract more than four million visitors a year.

1 **mumok**
The grey basalt lava building **(above)** is home to Europe's best collection of 20th-century masterpieces.

2 **ZOOM**
An exciting place **(below)** for kids aged eight months to 14 years. Children are encouraged to learn with fun, hands-on painting and activities *(see p69)*.

3 **Q21**
Vienna's centre for contemporary applied art, Q21 stages numerous creative initiatives that are spread all over the MQ. Street art and daily exhibitions, as well as office and editing spaces for the artists in residence, are among its programmes.

4 **Kunsthalle**
Considered the latest outpost of the contemporary art exhibition space on Karlsplatz *(see p59)*, Kunsthalle features frequently changing exhibitions of new artists.

9 Tanzquartier Wien

Known as TQW, this dance centre **(below)** is Austria's first dedicated performance and study venue focusing solely on modern dance.

6 Leopold Museum

The museum **(above)** has the world's biggest Egon Schiele collection, as well as paintings by Klimt.

7 Halle E+G

These two event halls host music, dance and musical theatre performances. The Baroque Halle E once housed horses.

8 wienXtra-kinderinfo

A play area for kids under 13 and information centre for parents, offering free advice on kids' activities in Vienna.

10 AzW

The Austrian Architecture Museum has exhibits, regular lectures and an extensive academic library, as well as an impressively designed restaurant in the complex.

MuseumsQuartier

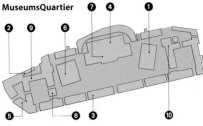

5 Dschungel

Vienna's theatre hub for kids and families features puppets, dance, film and even opera in two auditoriums.

NEED TO KNOW

MAP J5 ■ Museumsplatz 1 ■ 01 523 58 81 ■ www. mqw.at

mumok: open 2–7pm Mon, 10am–7pm Tue–Sun (until 9pm Thu); adm €11 (free entry for under 19s); www. mumok.at

ZOOM: open 8:30am–4pm Tue–Fri (Jul–Sep 12:45–5pm daily); www. kindermuseum.at

Q21: open 10am–10pm daily; www.q21.at

Kunsthalle: open 11am–7pm daily (to 9pm Thu); adm €12 (under 19s free); www.kunsthallewien.at

Dschungel: open 2:30–6:30pm Mon–Fri, 4:30–6:30pm Sat & Sun; adm €10; www.dschungelwien.at

Leopold Museum: open 10am–6pm daily (until 9pm Thu); adm €13; www.leopold.org

Halle E+G: open 10am–1pm & 2–7pm Mon–Sat; www.halleneg.at

wienXtra-kinderinfo: open 2–6pm Tue–Fri, 10am–5pm Sat & Sun; www.kinderinfo.wien.at

Tanzquartier Wien: open 9am–7:30pm Mon–Sat (from 10am Sat); adm €20; www.tqw.at

AzW: open 10am–7pm daily; adm €9 (under 6s free); www.azw.at

🔟 ⭐ Staatsoper

As the first of the grand buildings on the Ringstrasse, construction of the Neo-Renaissance State Opera House began in 1861 under the architects Eduard van der Nüll and August von Siccardsburg, and opened in May 1869 with Mozart's *Don Giovanni*. However, the new opera house did not appeal to Emperor Franz Joseph, who referred to it as a "railway station", leading van der Nüll to commit suicide. In 1945 the Staatsoper was hit by World War II bombs and almost entirely destroyed. Following its restoration in 1955, the State Opera is the world's largest repertory theatre. Performances are held 300 nights of the year.

6 Grand Staircase
The magnificent marble staircase (right), decorated with frescoes, mirrors and chandeliers, leads to the auditorium. In the arches are statues by Josef Gasser, illustrating the seven liberal arts: architecture, poetry, dance, sculpture, art, music and drama.

1 Exterior
Seen from the Ringstrasse, the majestic pale stone building is dominated by the original loggia, which survived World War II (above).

2 Bronze Statues
The large bronze statues, placed in the five arches of the loggia, are the creation of Ernst Julius Hähnel (1876) and are allegories of heroism, drama, fantasy, comedy and love, as seen from left to right.

3 Tea Salon
One of the most splendid rooms in the building is the Tea Salon. Its centrepiece is a fireplace flanked by pillars and mirrors.

4 Reliefs of Opera and Ballet
Created by Johann Preleuthner, two reliefs show the two genres performed in the house: opera and ballet.

5 Auditorium
Following its destruction in World War II, it was decided, after much discussion, that the auditorium be rebuilt to its original 1869 design with three box circles and two open circles (below).

7 Tapestries
Nine tapestries in the Gustav Mahler Hall, designed by Rudolf Eisenmenger, show scenes from Mozart's opera *The Magic Flute*.

10 Schwind Foyer

In the superb Schwind Foyer are 16 oil paintings by Moritz von Schwind. They represent some famous operas, including Rossini's *The Barber of Seville* (1816) and Beethoven's *Fidelio* (1805). A bust of the composers is placed beneath each illustration.

NEED TO KNOW

MAP M5 ■ Opernring 2 ■ 01 514 44 2606 (tours); 01 513 15 13 (tickets) ■ www.wiener-staatsoper.at

Open for pre-booked 40-minute guided tours only. Tour times vary and are usually scheduled around rehearsals

Adm €9

■ All tickets for the upcoming season can be booked in advance.

■ Up to 100 tickets at €15 are reserved for children under 14.

■ The ticket window sells tickets only for performances within the next two months.

■ Standing-room-only tickets are sold for as little as €5, 80 minutes before curtain time.

8 Gustav Mahler Bust

The bronze bust of composer Gustav Mahler, who was director of the Vienna Court Opera from 1897 to 1907, was created by Auguste Rodin in 1909. The bust is in the Schwind Foyer, along with the busts of other "conducting directors" of the opera.

9 Fountains

The two fountains that can be seen on the right and left sides of the opera house were created by the renowned Austrian sculptor Josef Gasser (1817–68). They represent two different worlds: music, dance, joy and levity on the left **(left)**, and the siren Lorelei with sorrow, love and revenge on the right.

📕🔟 ⭐ Secession Building

The large, white, cubic Secession Building was designed in 1897 by Joseph Maria Olbrich, the Austrian architect and co-founder of the Vienna Secession, as the manifesto of the late-19th-century art movement. The iconic exhibition hall opened in October 1898. The building was burned by retreating German forces during World War II and restoration began soon after in 1946. The upper floor was added in 1963 and comprehensive restoration to the original design took place between 1984 and 1985. Today it is one of the most treasured examples of a particularly Viennese artistic period.

1 Beethoven Frieze

Created by Gustav Klimt in 1902 for an exhibition paying homage to Ludwig van Beethoven, the 34-m- (110-ft-) long masterpiece of Viennese Art Nouveau **(above)** tells a story of the composer's Ninth Symphony, *Ode to Joy*.

2 Interior

The exhibition hall, in the shape of a basilica with a lofty nave and two lower aisles, can be easily adapted for each show staged here. Almost completely covered by a glass roof, by day it's bathed in a constant and even light.

3 Motto

Above the entrance of the pavilion is the gold motto of the Secessionist movement *"Der Zeit ihre Kunst. Der Kunst ihre Freiheit"* – "To every age its art, to art its freedom."

4 Flower Pots

The blue mosaic flowerpots on either side of the entrance door are carried by four turtles. Their small trees add a touch of nature to smooth the building's hard lines **(right)**.

5 Mark Anthony Statue

The bronze sculpture of the Roman general Mark Anthony in a chariot drawn by lions was created by Arthur Strasser in 1898. It was displayed at the fourth exhibition in the Secession and then set outside the building.

6 Dome

Made of 2,500 gilt laurel leaves and 311 berries, the dome is the most prominent feature of the design. The laurel symbolizes victory, dignity and purity.

7 Façade

Due to its huge, unbroken walls, the building appears to be constructed from solid cubes **(above)**.

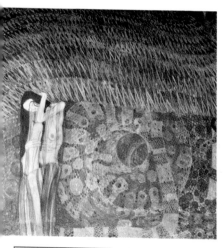

8 Ornaments

The building is decorated with gilt laurel garlands, floral patterns and plants along the sides of the walls. Most striking is the gold tree above the main door. These details contrast strikingly with the simplistic façade.

UNVEILING THE SECESSION

The sober functionalism of the Secession Building was regarded with horror and widely condemned when it was completed in 1898. Critics called it "a public convenience", "a greenhouse" and "a warehouse" and said it was an assault on good taste. Today, however, it is regarded as one of the key works of the Viennese Art Nouveau style and the residents of Vienna are proud of "their" building, which is affectionately called "the golden cabbage" because of its dome.

9 Architecture

The ground plan of the pavilion reveals simple geometrical forms, taking the square as the basic shape. The framework is softened by curves and ornaments.

10 Gorgons' Heads

The entrance is decorated with the heads of the three Gorgons **(below)**, which represent architecture, sculpture and painting. The sides also feature owls which, with the Gorgons, are virtues of Pallas Athena, Greek goddess of wisdom, victory and the crafts.

TOP 10 ⭐ **Hundertwasserhaus**

Opened in March 1986, this fairy-tale house with onion spires, green roof and a multicoloured façade is one of the city's most visited landmarks. Flamboyant Austrian artist Friedensreich Hundertwasser designed it as a playful take on usually dull social housing. In all his work Hundertwasser wanted to show that practical could also be beautiful. Today almost 200 people live in the 50 apartments, each of which is individually decorated. Shrubs and trees on the balconies and roof gardens bring nature closer to city dwellers.

Façade ①
The front of the house **(right)** is painted in bright shades of blue, yellow, red and white, and each of the differently coloured sections marks one apartment. The many trees growing in the rooftop gardens of the apartment block are also very unusual.

② **Main Entrance**
The building's main entrance, situated on Löwengasse, is an open section leading to the inner courtyard of the building. The apartments set just above the main entrance are supported by colourful pillars. In front of the entrance is an attractive small fountain **(above)**.

NEED TO KNOW

Kegelgasse 36–38
■ U-Bahn Landstrasse or trams 1 or O to Löwengasse or 4A to Marxergasse ■ www.das-hundertwasser-haus.at

■ The apartments are private residences and can't be visited, but you can enjoy the building from one of the cafés in the complex, and stroll around the shops on the ground floor.

3 Onion Towers
Two golden glistening onion towers sit atop the Hundertwasserhaus and lend the building an Oriental, romantic quality **(above)**.

4 Irregular Windows
Hundertwasser believed that windows constitute a house's soul, so all the windows here vary in size and shape, and each of them is framed by a complementary colour.

7 Decorations
The building is decorated with black, white and golden tiles. Statues on the corners of balconies, painted animals and plants on the corridor walls, and roof gardens give the place a cheerful appearance.

5 Roof Gardens
Each apartment has access to a little piece of nature in the form of the roof gardens and balconies that are scattered all over the building. The gardens have some 250 large trees, trimmed shrubs and a grass lawn.

6 Ceramic Line
The size of every apartment is visible as it's marked by an uneven line of ceramic tiles **(below)**.

FRIEDENSREICH HUNDERTWASSER

When Friedensreich Hundertwasser (1928–2000) left the Vienna Academy of Fine Arts in 1948 after only three months of study, it was hard to imagine that he would one day become one of Austria's most acclaimed artists and a master of design for everything from stamps and coins to buildings and paintings. Bright colours contrasted by black and gold, and the spiral, which he used in his work to symbolize the beginning and end of life, gradually became his artistic trademarks. His aim was to create architecture in harmony with nature and man.

8 Pillars
A prominent feature of the structure is the range of brightly coloured, irregularly shaped shiny pillars **(above)**. Some of these pillars are integrated in the building and function as mere decoration, while others are more practical and are used to support the gallery that runs along the first floor of the block.

9 Glass Front
The two towers of the house – those crowned by the onion domes – host the central staircase. Thanks to the glass fronts, by day they are always light and airy.

10 Pavement
The area around Löwengasse is pedestrianized with some relaxed seating and elegant lampposts.

TOP 10 ⭐ Schloss Schönbrunn

The former summer residence of the Habsburgs, Schönbrunn Palace was built on land acquired by Maximilian II in 1569. At that time it was a wooded area outside the city. During the Turkish Siege of 1683, however, the woodland was destroyed, clearing the ground for this spectacular palace, built between 1695 and 1713 to the designs of the architect Johann Fischer von Erlach. Little of his original plans remains – Empress Maria Theresa ordered most of the interior to be redesigned in Late Baroque, or Rococo, style. The façade was altered in 1817–19, when it was painted in the characteristic "Schönbrunn yellow".

1 Grand Gallery
The 40-m- (130-ft-) long, 10-m- (30-ft-) wide gallery (above) has a stunning Rococo design of tall windows, splendid crystal mirrors, chandeliers and white-and-gold stucco. The Grand Gallery is still used for state receptions and banquets.

2 Porcelain Room
Maria Theresa's former study walls are covered with carved wooden frames painted blue and white to imitate porcelain.

3 Vieux-Laque Room
This room (left) unites Rococo elements with Chinese art: lacquer panels show landscapes adorned in gold. After her husband Francis I died in 1765, Maria Theresa hung portraits of him here as a memorial.

Schloss Schönbrunn

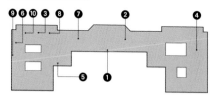

⑩ Napoleon's Room

When Napoleon occupied Vienna in 1805 and 1809 he stayed in this splendid room. Flemish tapestries from the 18th century adorn the walls.

④ Empress Elisabeth Salon

In Empress Elisabeth's Neo-Rococo reception room, there are portraits of Emperor Joseph I as a child and his sister Marie Antoinette.

⑤ Chapel

In 1740 Maria Theresa remodelled the chapel. The marble altar was designed by Georg Raphael Donner, and Paul Troger painted the ceiling fresco *The Marriage of the Virgin*.

⑥ Millions' Room

The name derives from the room's rosewood panelling, which cost a reputed one million Gulden (former Austrian gold coins). In the panels, Indo-Persian miniatures illustrate scenes from the lives of the Mogul rulers of India in the 16th and 17th centuries.

⑧ Blue Chinese Salon

Blue rice-paper wallpaper, Japanese vases and pieces of lacquer furniture create an Oriental theme here **(below)**.

⑨ Mirror Room

With magnificent white-and-gold Rococo decoration and crystal mirrors, this room is a fine example of Maria Theresa's style. Mozart once gave a private performance for the empress here.

⑦ Bergl Rooms

The garden rooms were painted with frescoes by Johann Wenzl Bergl (1768–77) to satisfy Maria Theresa's taste for exotic landscapes **(above)**.

NEED TO KNOW

Schönbrunner Schloss Strasse 47 ▪ U-Bahn Schönbrunn ▪ 01 811 13 239 ▪ www.schoenbrunn.at

Palace: open 8am–dusk daily; adm €14.20 (22 rooms), €17.50 (40 rooms), €20.50 (with tour guide)

Grand Park: 6:30am–dusk daily

Privy, Orangery, Maze and Gloriette: 9am–dusk daily; adm €3.80 for each, maze €5.50

Children's Museum: 10am–5pm Sat & Sun (daily during school hols); adm €8.80

▪ On the ground floor of the west wing, the Children's Museum allows kids to dress up as Habsburgs (www.kaiserkinder.at).

▪ There are several admission prices and combination passes for the complex, depending on how many sights you want to visit.

Palace Guide

Enter through the main gate and head to the left wing, where you can buy tickets for visiting the interior and pick up a map of the palace and grounds. The carriage museum, palm house and zoo are to the right of the palace *(see pp44–5)*. Behind the palace are flowerbeds laid out in Baroque style.

Features of Schönbrunn's Gardens

1 **Schlosstheater**
Commissioned by Maria Theresa, the theatre opened in 1747. The empress and her many children performed on the stage as singers.

2 **Palmenhaus**
The stunning steel-and-glass palm house was built in 1881–2 by Franz Xavier Segenschmid, using the latest technology. The central pavilion is 28 m (90 ft) high and has two wings.

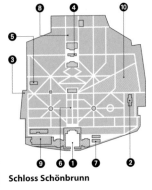

Schloss Schönbrunn

Schönbrunn's Palmenhaus

3 **Roman Ruins**
Built in 1778, the Roman Ruins were designed to enhance the prestige and image of the Habsburgs by presenting them as the successors to the heroic Roman emperors.

4 **Gloriette**
Situated at the summit of the park's hill, the magnificent Gloriette is its most prominent feature. The arcaded edifice was designed by Ferdinand Hetzendorf von Hohenberg in 1775 in Neo-Classical style and was once used as a dining hall before it became a viewing point, then later a café.

5 **Beautiful Fountain**
A fresh spring was discovered by Emperor Matthias while hunting in the area in 1619. In 1630, a well, together with a statue of a Roman nymph, was placed here, and it gave the palace its name (Schönbrunn is German for "beautiful fountain"). The fountain is close to the Roman Ruins.

6 **Mythological Statues**
The large park is dotted with 32 stone statues, created by Christian Beyer between 1753 and 1775. Each one represents a figure in Greek mythology or Roman history.

7 **Wagenburg**
A highlight of the Wagenburg (carriage museum) is the richly decorated imperial coach, which was built for the coronation of Joseph II in 1765. It was so heavy that eight horses were needed to pull it at walking pace.

The distinctive Gloriette arcade

EMPRESS MARIA THERESA AND SCHLOSS SCHÖNBRUNN

Most of the palace as it appears today was created during the reign of Empress Maria Theresa. She ascended the throne in 1740 after her father Charles VI changed the succession to enable females to rule Habsburg countries. The early years of her reign were characterized by foreign political failures as parts of Poland and Italy were lost in wars. But in domestic politics she introduced compulsory education, set up a new administrative structure and improved the social situation for farmers. Maria Theresa was impulsive in her younger years, but after the death of her husband Francis I in 1765 she wore only black mourning gowns and lived a sombre existence. She gave birth to 16 children, 10 of whom survived into adulthood.

TOP 10 RESIDENTS OF SCHLOSS SCHÖNBRUNN

1 Charles VI (1685–1740)

2 Maria Theresa (1717–80)

3 Francis I, husband of Maria Theresa (1708–65)

4 Marie Antoinette spent an idyllic childhood at Schönbrunn (1755–93)

5 Napoleon (1769–1821) used the palace as his headquarters in 1805 and 1809

6 Marie Louise, wife of Napoleon I (1791–1847)

7 Franz Josef Karl, Duke of Reichstadt, known as Napoleon II (1811–32)

8 Franz Joseph was born and died in the palace (1830–1916)

9 Elisabeth, wife of Franz Joseph (1837–98)

10 Rudolph (1858–89)

This portrait of Empress Maria Theresa by Josef Kiss and Friedrich Mayrhofer was painted in 1740, the year of her ascension to the throne.

8 Schönbrunn Park

The formal French Baroque park was laid out as a large pleasure garden by Nicolaus Jadot and Adrian von Steckhoven during the reign of Maria Theresa. It includes various architectural features.

9 Orangery

Schönbrunn's gardens are home to the second-largest Baroque orangery in the world. It was once used as winter quarters for orange trees and other potted plants, as well as for various imperial festivities.

10 Schönbrunn Zoo

Founded as early as 1752 as a royal menagerie by Emperor Franz I, this is the world's oldest zoo and is home to some 750 species.

Flamingos at Schönbrunn Zoo

The Top 10 of Everything

**Detail of the Art Nouveau altar
at Kirche am Steinhof**

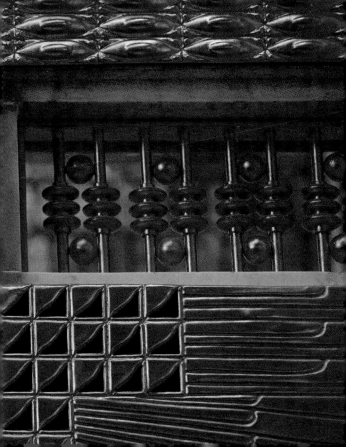

🔟 Moments in History

1 Early Vienna
Early settlements in the area date back to the late Stone Age (5000 BC). The Celts later established the kingdom of Noricum in 200 BC. This was conquered by the Romans in 15 BC, who later set up a garrison, Vindobona, in AD 100.

2 Babenberg Rule
In AD 976 the Babenberg ruler Leopold was appointed Duke of the Eastern March, and in 1030 the name "Vienna" was used for the first time. In 1156 Vienna became the main residence of the Babenbergs and developed into a centre of trade.

3 Habsburg Rule
After the death of the last Babenberg and a period of social disorder, the Habsburg Rudolph I was elected king in 1273. Vienna became the de facto centre of the Holy Roman Empire and an important centre for arts, science and music. It remained the imperial city of the Habsburgs until 1918.

Stained-glass window of Rudolph I

4 Turkish Siege
After Turkish troops failed to conquer Vienna in 1529, a huge army returned in 1683. The city was under siege for three months, but was liberated with the help of Polish troops. Prince Eugene finally destroyed the Ottoman Empire's influence with his victory in Belgrade in 1717.

5 Vienna Congress
After Napoleon was defeated in Leipzig (1813), the European powers met in Vienna in 1814–15 to make territorial decisions. The congress was attended by high-ranking delegates and glamorous balls were held.

6 1848 Revolution
A rigid political system under the state chancellor Metternich led to a period of calm and a rich cultural life (1815–48), but social discontent returned and led to political upheaval in 1848. Upheavals reached a peak in October. Metternich was ousted from power and liberal ministers were appointed.

Painting of Vienna burning during the revolution in October 1848

7 End of the Austro-Hungarian Empire

With the death of Franz Joseph I in 1916, the Austro-Hungarian monarchy lost its uniting figure. Charles I, his successor, was not able to secure peace. The empire's defeat in World War I resulted in the Habsburgs losing both their lands and their crown.

8 First Republic

When a new European map was drawn in 1918 at the end of World War I, the small Republic of Austria emerged. However, the country was struggling both economically and politically. Social unrest led to a civil war in February 1934, followed by a period of authoritarian rule.

German forces entering Vienna in 1938

9 Anschluss

Adolf Hitler marched on Vienna in March 1938 and declared Austria part of the Third Reich. Vienna was badly bombed during World War II, with many iconic landmarks destroyed.

10 Second Republic

In 1945, at the end of World War II, Vienna was divided into four zones occupied by the Allied powers (Great Britain, France, Russia and the US). In 1955, the last Allied soldiers left the country, and Austria regained full sovereignty with the signing of the State Treaty in May (see p29).

TOP 10 FAMOUS EMPERORS AND EMPRESSES

Empress Maria Theresa

1 Rudolph I
Rudolph (1273–91) began the Habsburg rule in Austria.

2 Friedrich III
The motto of Friedrich III (1440–93) was AEIOU – *Alle Erde ist Österreichs Untertan"* (All Earth Is Austria's Subject).

3 Maximilian I
Under this Renaissance ruler (1486–1519), all Habsburg lands were united and the arts and sciences flourished.

4 Charles VI
Charles VI (1711–40) changed the rules of succession, allowing females to ascend the throne.

5 Maria Theresa
Maria Theresa (1740–80), known for her strong Catholic beliefs, modernized the empire by introducing many reforms.

6 Joseph II
Known as a tolerant ruler, Joseph II (1765–90) carried out further reforms started under his mother Maria Theresa.

7 Franz II
As the last Emperor of the Holy Roman Empire, the Napoleonic Wars and Vienna Congress came under the reign of Franz II (1792–1835).

8 Franz Joseph I
He came to power aged 18 and epitomized the monarchy as no other emperor before him (1848–1916).

9 Sisi
Married at 16 to Franz Joseph I, the youthful Empress Elisabeth (1854–98) was assassinated in Geneva.

10 Charles I
As the last of the Habsburg monarchs (1916–18), Charles I was forced to leave the country in exile in 1918.

⓽⓾ Palaces and Historic Buildings

Baroque Gartenpalais Liechtenstein

① Gartenpalais Liechtenstein

At the end of the 17th century the Liechtenstein family commissioned various architects to build them a summer residence. This impressive Baroque building has been renovated and now houses the private art collection of the Liechtenstein family (mainly 17th-century art) *(see p101)*.

② Palais Pallavicini
MAP M4 ■ Josefsplatz 5 ■ Closed to the public

Built between 1782 and 1784, this was Vienna's first Neo-Classical building, imitating ancient Greek as well as Roman architecture. The formal façade is enlivened by the impressive portal with caryatids by Franz Anton von Zauner. The Pallavicini family still live here, and parts of the palace host a congress centre.

③ Augartenpalais
MAP B5 ■ Obere Augartenstrasse 1–3 ■ Closed to the public

The Baroque palace in Augarten park is now the home of the Vienna Boys' Choir school.

④ Palais Lobkowitz
MAP M4 ■ Lobkowitzplatz 2 ■ Open 10am–6pm Wed–Mon ■ Adm

This large Baroque palace was designed by Giovanni Pietro Tencalla in 1685 as a stately city mansion for Count Dietrichstein. The Lobkowitz family acquired the palace in 1753. The building currently hosts the fabulous Paintings Gallery of the Academy of Fine Arts, as well as the Austrian Theatre Museum.

⑤ Palais Schönborn-Batthyány
MAP L2 ■ Renngasse 4 ■ Closed to the public

The palace, designed by Fischer von Erlach between 1699 and 1706, was the home of the Hungarian Batthyány family, who fought for Prince Eugene *(see p48)*. The Schönborns acquired it in 1740; today it hosts classical music events.

⑥ Palais Ferstel
MAP L2 ■ Strauchgasse 4 ■ Closed to the public

This grand building in Historicist style was constructed between 1856 and 1860 by Heinrich Ferstel as a stock exchange for the National Bank. Now part of the palace is the Café Central *(see p98)*. The building is sometimes used for gala events.

Gilded arcade in Palais Ferstel

Dorotheum
The grand palace, built in Neo-Baroque style between 1898 and 1901 by Emil Ritter von Förster, hosts pawnshops and one of Europe's largest auction houses *(see p97)*.

8 Palais Daun-Kinsky
MAP L2 ■ Freyung 4

This is Baroque architect Johann Lukas von Hildebrandt's most splendid palace (1713–16). The Kinsky family purchased it in 1784. Today, the lavish state rooms are used for weddings and dinner events.

Lavish dining at Palais Daun-Kinsky

 Palais Trautson
MAP J4 ■ Museumstrasse 7
■ Closed to the public

Count Trautson had this palace built in 1710–17 in French style; Maria Theresa converted it into guards' headquarters in 1760. Today it is used by the Austrian Justice Ministry.

 Palais Mollard-Clary
MAP L2 ■ Herrengasse 9

This 17th-century five-storey family mansion in the Baroque style was used by Joseph II for his famous round table soirées. It now houses the Austrian National Library, as well as the Globe Museum *(see p67)*.

TOP 10 EXAMPLES OF ARCHITECTURAL STYLES

1 Roman Houses
MAP L3 ■ Michaelerplatz
Early houses in parts of central Vienna were built by the Roman garrisons.

2 Medieval House
MAP P3 ■ Schönlaterngasse 7
The Basiliskenhaus is a fine example of a 13th-century home.

3 Renaissance
MAP N2 ■ Salvatorgasse 5
The portal of the Salvatorkapelle church dates back to 1530.

4 Baroque Palaces
Palaces built in richly decorated Baroque style can be found throughout Vienna, especially around the Ringstrasse.

5 Biedermeier House
MAP N5 ■ Annagasse 11
Arabesques and frescoes are typical of the Biedermeier period (1815–1848).

6 Art Nouveau Buildings
The stations of the former city railway were constructed by Otto Wagner in the 1890s *(see p122)*.

7 Purist Villa
Starkfriedgasse 19 ■ Bus 41A
The symmetrical Villa Moller by Adolf Loos (1917) reflects his principles of the use of space.

8 Council Housing
Heiligenstädter Strasse 82–92
■ U-Bahn U4, U6
The massive Karl-Marx-Hof building was constructed in 1930.

9 Haas-Haus
Designed by Hans Hollein in 1990, this building is part-mirrored *(see p95)*.

10 Gasometer
These gas storage towers were turned into apartments in 2001 *(see p66)*.

Gasometer apartment block

🔟 Monuments and Memorials

① Johann Strauss Monument

MAP P5 ▪ Stadtpark, Parkring

Stadtpark (see p62) is dotted with monuments of artists and composers, but the gilded 1921 statue of Johann Strauss is allegedly the city's most photographed. The Viennese "Waltz King" is shown playing the violin amid ecstatic dancers and is framed by a marble arch.

Johann Strauss Monument, Stadtpark

② Schubert's Grave

Zentralfriedhof, Simmeringer Hauptstrasse 234 ▪ Tram 71

Franz Schubert was buried at the Währinger Friedhof on 21 November 1828, following his early death aged 31. When the cemetery was closed in 1872, his bones were moved to the Central Cemetery. There he was given an honorary grave among many of his composer friends.

③ Franz Schubert Monument

MAP Q4 ▪ Stadtpark, Parkring

Franz Schubert is also commemorated with a monument in Stadtpark. It was commissioned by the men's choir Wiener Männergesangsverein, and was created by Carl Kundmann in 1872.

④ Memorial against War and Fascism

MAP M5 ▪ Albertinaplatz

The Austrian sculptor Alfred Hrdlicka created a monument in 1988–91 to commemorate all those killed during the National Socialist regime and World War II. Separate elements, made of granite from the area of the Mauthausen concentration camp, are arranged on the square where the Philipphof house was situated. The house was destroyed during an air raid on 12 March 1945 and more than 300 people were buried alive in its debris. The Proclamation of the Second Austrian Republic is carved on the "Stone of the Republic" here.

⑤ Mariensäule Am Hof

MAP M2 ▪ Am Hof

Am Hof is dominated by a monument to the Virgin Mary that was cast in bronze by Balthasar Herold (1664–7). The base shows four angels fighting with four animals, which symbolize the four major catastrophes for humankind in the 17th century. The dragon stands for starvation, the lion for war, the fantastical basilisk for the plague, while a snake represents the catastrophe of heresy.

⑥ Goethe Monument

MAP L5 ▪ Opernring/ Goethegasse

Next to the Burggarten is a large monument to one of the greatest writers in the German language, Johann Wolfgang von Goethe. The statue, seated on a massive base and cast in bronze, was created by Austrian sculptor Edmund von Hellmer in 1900. Opposite the monument is a memorial to another distinguished German writer and Goethe's contemporary, Friedrich Schiller (see p116).

Goethe Monument

The Maria Theresa Monument in front of the Naturhistorisches Museum

(7) Maria Theresa Monument

MAP K5 ■ Maria-Theresien-Platz

Between the Kunsthistorisches and Naturhistorisches museums is a statue of Empress Maria Theresa (1717–80). The German sculptor Kaspar von Zumbusch created the elaborate monument in 1888, presenting the empress seated on the throne surrounded by ministers and advisors, as well as composers such as Mozart and Haydn.

(8) Klimt's Grave

Hietzinger Friedhof, Maxingstrasse 15 ■ U-Bahn U4

The grave of the leading Secessionist painter Gustav Klimt (see p31) is in the Hietzinger Cemetery, close to Schloss Schönbrunn. Klimt's simple gravestone bears his name in the way he signed his works of art. He died in 1918 following a stroke.

(9) Schönberg's Grave

Zentralfriedhof, Simmeringer Hauptstrasse 234 ■ Tram 71

The composer Arnold Schönberg (1874–1951), creator of the 12-tone serial music technique (see p61), has a striking modern cube as his gravestone. It was designed by the Austrian sculptor Fritz Wotruba.

(10) Mahler's Grave

Grinzinger Friedhof, An den langen Lüssen 33 ■ Train Grinzing

Gustav Mahler, director of the Vienna State Opera from 1897 to 1907, was buried at the Grinzinger Friedhof in 1911. The cemetery is in a peaceful location on the outskirts of the city. Mahler's simple white gravestone was designed by his friend, the architect and designer Josef Hoffmann.

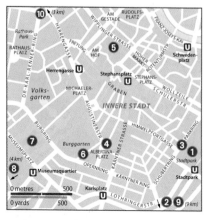

Top10 Places of Worship

The lavish pink and gold Baroque interior of Jesuitenkirche

1 Griechisch-Orthodoxe Kirche

MAP N2 ■ Fleischmarkt 13

In the early 18th century a Greek Orthodox community was founded in Vienna. After Emperor Joseph II issued a tolerance decree in 1787, the church on Fleischmarkt was built by Danish architect Theophil von Hansen. The pretty gold-and-red-striped building with arched windows was altered in Byzantine style in the mid-1900s.

2 Jesuitenkirche

MAP P3 ■ Doktor-Ignaz-Seipel-Platz 1

Constructed at the beginning of the 17th century, the solemn façade of the Jesuitenkirche contrasts with its rich Baroque interior. Emperor Leopold I commissioned the Italian architect Andrea Pozzo to design the magnificent frescoes and paintings housed within the church. Pozzo also painted the barrel-vaulted ceiling so that the illusion of a dome was created.

3 Stephansdom

Sitting in the very heart of the city, this spectacular Gothic cathedral dominates the skyline (see pp12–15).

4 Karlskirche

This stunning domed church combines Oriental and Baroque flourishes (see pp32–3).

5 Votivkirche

The impressive sandstone church in Neo-Gothic style was built between 1855 and 1879

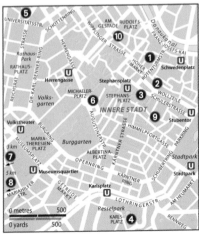

to express gratitude that Franz Joseph survived an assassination attempt in 1853 (see p102).

6 Michaelerkirche
MAP M3 ▪ Michaelerplatz ▪ Guided tours of the crypt 11am & 1pm Thu–Sat ▪ Adm

The imperial court attended masses in this church opposite the Hofburg palace. Originally Romanesque, it changed in style over the centuries after being rebuilt several times due to damage by fire. The original stone helmet of the tower, damaged after an earthquake, was replaced by a pointed roof in 1590. The portal is Baroque (1724–5) and the interior is dominated by Romanesque arcades and a Baroque high altar.

7 Kirche am Steinhof
This fine Art Nouveau church (see p127) was designed by Otto Wagner and built in 1905–7 on the grounds of a psychiatric hospital. The square-shaped church with two bell towers and four angels over the door is overlooked by a golden dome that was converted to copper in the 1930s but has more recently been restored to its traditional hues. The window mosaics, designed by Kolo Moser, and a gilt altar canopy with angels delight those who enter the interior.

Art Nouveau Kirche am Steinhof

8 Wotruba-Kirche
Georgsgasse, corner of Rysergasse ▪ Bus 60A

This unconventional church was built between 1974 and 1976 following designs by the Austrian sculptor Fritz Wotruba, who died shortly before the work was finished. It consists of 157 concrete cubes in various sizes that form a harmonious whole. In the spaces between the cubes, glass panes flood the interior with daylight.

The unusual Wotruba-Kirche

9 Franziskanerkirche
MAP N4 ▪ Franziskanerplatz

Located on the Franziskanerplatz (see p94), the church and adjacent monastery of the Franciscan Order were constructed between 1603 and 1611 on the site of an older church. Dedicated to St Jerome, it is the city's only religious building with a Renaissance façade, but it also bears some Gothic and Baroque features, including six side altars in ornate recesses and a fine Baroque high altar of 1707 by Andrea Pozzo.

10 Maria am Gestade
MAP M2 ▪ Salvatorgasse 12

This Gothic church, constructed on the site of a former wooden chapel, has an impressively slim west front, just 33 m (108 ft) high and only 10 m (30 ft) wide. The tower is crowned by a white, open stone helmet (1394–1414) that once served as a landmark for Danube mariners. In a state of decay in the late 18th century, it was used as stables during the Napoleonic Wars but was restored in 1812.

🔟 Museums

Aircraft on display at the Technisches Museum Wien

① Technisches Museum Wien

Mariahilfer Strasse 212 ■ **U-Bahn Schönbrunn; Tram 52, 58** ■ **Open 9am–6pm Mon–Fri, 10am–6pm Sat, Sun** ■ **Adm (free for under 19s)** ■ **www.technischesmuseum.at**

Opened in 1918, this museum houses more than 80,000 exhibits relating to technology, energy and heavy industry.

② Camera and Photography Museum Westlicht

MAP E1 ■ **Westbahnstrasse 40** ■ **Open 11am–7pm daily (to 9pm Thu)** ■ **Adm** ■ **www.westlicht.com**

Around 800 cameras are on display, including KGB spy cameras disguised as cigarette packets or evening bags.

③ Erzbischöfliches Dom- und Diözesanmuseum

MAP N3 ■ **Stephansplatz 6** ■ **Open 10am–6pm Wed–Sun (to 8pm Thu)** ■ **Adm** ■ **www.dommuseum.at**

Located in the Archbishop's Palace, this museum displays an impressive selection of precious religious art, including 9th-century manuscripts.

④ Mozarthaus Vienna

MAP N3 ■ **Domgasse 5** ■ **Open 10am–7pm daily** ■ **Adm** ■ **www.mozarthausvienna.at**

Mozart occupied a flat on the first floor of the Figarohaus in 1784–7. He composed some of his masterworks here, including *The Marriage of Figaro*. The museum has exhibitions as well as Mozart's first-floor flat *(see p61)*.

⑤ Museum für angewandte Kunst (MAK)

MAP Q3 ■ **Stubenring 5** ■ **Open 10am–6pm Tue–Sun (to 10pm Tue)** ■ **Adm (free 6–10pm Tue and for under 19s)** ■ **www.mak.at**

The Austrian Museum of Applied Arts includes world-famous works by the Wiener Werkstätte, an arts and crafts studio from 1870 to 1956.

⑥ Naturhistorisches Museum

Especially enthralling for families, the fascinating Natural History Museum *(see p107)* is world-class, both for its fascinating collection, as well as its architecture.

Naturhistorisches Museum

7 Heergeschichtliches Museum

Arsenal, Objekt 18 ▪ Bus 69A, 13A; Tram O, D, 18 ▪ Open 9am–5pm daily ▪ Adm (free for under 19s and first Sun of month) ▪ www.hgm.or.at

The Museum of Military History documents the imperial army from the 16th century to 1918.

8 Jüdisches Museum der Stadt Wien

MAP M4 ▪ Palais Eskeles, Dorotheergasse 11 ▪ Open 10am–6pm Sun–Fri ▪ Adm (free for under 18s) ▪ www.jmw.at

The world's first Jewish museum was founded in Vienna in 1895, but the exhibits were confiscated by National Socialists in 1938. The present museum, housed in the Palais Eskeles, has a library and archives. Nearby, another museum, at Judenplatz, displays excavations of a medieval synagogue.

Stairwell in the Haus der Musik

9 Haus der Musik

MAP N5 ▪ Seilerstätte 30 ▪ Open 10am–10pm daily ▪ Adm ▪ www.hdm.at

At the House of Music visitors are invited to experiment with sounds, to play giant instruments or to "conduct" the Vienna Philharmonic Orchestra.

10 Wien Museum Karlsplatz

MAP F5 ▪ Karlsplatz ▪ Open 10am–6pm Tue–Sun & public hols ▪ Adm (free for under 19s and first Sun of month) ▪ Free guided tours ▪ www.wienmuseum.at

Set over three storeys, this museum documents the history of Vienna with items spanning 7,000 years.

TOP 10 UNUSUAL MUSEUMS

Exhibits at the Clownmuseum

1 Clownmuseum
Ilgplatz 7
A collection of colourful circus posters, props, costumes and programmes.

2 Fiakermuseum
Veronikagasse 12
A museum dedicated to the Viennese horse-drawn carriages known as *fiaker*.

3 Kriminalmuseum
MAP B5 ▪ Sperlgasse 24
Shows the city's most sensational crimes, from the Middle Ages to the present.

4 Schnapsmuseum
Wilhelmstrasse 19–21
Set in an old distillery, this museum is devoted to the Austrian drink, schnapps.

5 Uhrenmuseum
MAP M2 ▪ Schulhof 2
Timepieces of all ages and shapes.

6 Josephinum
A collection of anatomical wax models once used to train surgeons *(see p102)*.

7 Pathologisch-Anatomisches Museum
MAP B2 ▪ Vienna University Campus, Spitalgasse 2
A former psychiatric ward houses a morbid collection of medical horrors.

8 Third Man Museum
MAP F3 ▪ Pressgasse 25
A museum dedicated to the 1949 classic movie *The Third Man*, filmed in Vienna.

9 Bestattungsmuseum
This undertakers' museum in Vienna's Zentralfriedhof (Central Cemetery) shows all kinds of funereal objects *(see p67)*.

10 Kaffeemuseum
MAP H3 ▪ Vogelsanggasse 36, A-10
This small museum celebrates coffee, the favourite drink of the Viennese.

🔟 Art Galleries

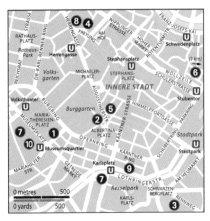

The Upper Belvedere displays art from the Middle Ages onwards while the Lower Belvedere houses temporary exhibitions (see pp28–31).

4 Kunstforum Bank Austria

MAP L2 ■ Freyung 8 ■ Open 10am–7pm daily (to 9pm Fri) ■ Adm ■ www.kunstforumwien.at

Dedicated to the modern classics and their forerunners, the Kunstforum organizes several major exhibitions a year. By presenting shows of world-famous artists such as Egon Schiele, Oskar Kokoschka, Paul Cézanne, Pablo Picasso and Vincent van Gogh, the gallery is a magnet for visitors and has always attracted large crowds of art lovers.

5 Akademie der bildenden Künste Picture Collection

The painting gallery of the Academy of Fine Arts has moved to Palais Lobkowitz (see p50) due to restoration work at the school on Schillerplatz (see p115). Among its masterpieces are paintings by Titian, Rembrandt, Ruben and the Last Judgement (1500) by Hieronymus Bosch.

6 KunstHaus Wien

Untere Weissgerberstrasse 13 ■ U-Bahn Landstrasse; Tram O, 1 ■ Open 10am–6pm daily ■ Adm ■ www.kunsthauswien.com

The world's only permanent collection of the works of the Austrian artist Friedensreich Hundertwasser, the gallery is privately funded and receives almost 200,000 visitors a year. Located near the famous Hundertwasserhaus (see pp40–41), the museum's black-and-white façade, uneven floors and roof gardens were designed by the artist himself in 1989.

1 Kunsthistorisches Museum

The impressive imperial art collection is housed in the Kunsthistorisches Museum and includes one of the world's finest gatherings of works by the Old Masters (see pp22–5).

Interior of the Albertina palace

2 Albertina

The Albertina palace houses a collection of graphic art, architectural drawings and photographs from all periods. The 65,000 drawings and almost one million prints include works by Dürer and Klimt (see p91).

3 The Belvedere

This Baroque palace is home to a wonderful collection of Austrian artworks, including paintings by Gustav Klimt and Egon Schiele.

Sculpture on display at the Kunsthalle

7 Kunsthalle
MAP J5 & MAP F4
■ **Museumsplatz 1 & Treitlstrasse 2**
■ **Open 11am–7pm daily (to 9pm Thu)** ■ Adm ■ www.kunsthallewien.at

The Kunsthalle has two venues – one within the MuseumsQuartier *(see p34)* and one at Karlsplatz. This means that there is lots of space for changing exhibitions. The Kunsthalle specializes in contemporary art. At the Karlsplatz site, the exhibits can be seen from the outside, as the building is a glass cube.

8 Museum im Schottenstift
MAP L2 ■ **Freyung 6** ■ **Open 11am–5pm Tue–Sat (closed public hols)** ■ Adm ■ www.schotten.wien

The Scots' Abbey, founded in 1155 by Scottish and Irish Benedictine monks, is a massive complex, containing a church, a school and a monastery. The abbey's stunning treasures include tapestries, furniture and many liturgical objects. Most important of all are the museum's religious landscape and portrait paintings from all periods.

9 Künstlerhaus
MAP N6 ■ **Karlsplatz 5** ■ **Open 10am–6pm daily (to 9pm Thu)** ■ Adm ■ www.k-haus.at

Back in its original historic location, this unique institution for graphic artists is closed for renovations until September 2018. Built between 1865 and 1868, the grand white stone edifice retains its Italian Renaissance style, but inside it has been updated to the latest in museum technology, with frequent experimental displays of video and laser projections.

10 mumok
The official name of this gallery is the Museum Moderner Kunst Stiftung Ludwig Wien. It contains one of the largest European collections of modern and contemporary art, from American Pop Art, Photo Realism, Fluxus and Nouveau Réalism to Viennese Actionism, Arte Povera, Conceptual and Minimal Art. The galleries are split chronologically over five levels, two underground. Tours in English are held at 4pm on Saturdays *(see p34)*.

mumok, MuseumsQuartier

⭐10 Composers

1 Joseph Haydn

Along with Beethoven and Mozart, Haydn (1732–1809) is the third important composer of the Vienna Classical period (1770–1830). He moved to Vienna aged eight, to become a choirboy at Stephansdom. In his house at Haydngasse 19 he wrote his greatest works, such as the oratory *The Creation* (1796–8).

2 Wolfgang Amadeus Mozart

Although born in Salzburg, the life of this world-famous composer (1756–91) is inextricably intertwined with Vienna. Mozart moved to the city in 1781 after falling out with his sponsor, the Archbishop of Salzburg. It was here that he wrote his greatest works and celebrated all his triumphs and misfortunes until he died, aged 35.

Portrait of Franz Schubert

4 Franz Schubert

The twelfth child born in the family home at Nussdorfer Strasse 54 in Vienna, Franz Schubert (1797–1828) composed many symphonies, although it is for his songs that he is best remembered.

5 Anton Bruckner

Born in a small town to the northwest of Vienna, Bruckner (1824–96) moved to the capital in 1868, when he became a professor at the city's musical academy. Well respected today, his contemporaries were critical about his music and some of his pieces were never performed during his lifetime.

Manuscript handwritten by Mozart

3 Ludwig van Beethoven

When Ludwig van Beethoven (1770–1827) gave his first concert in the Vienna Court Theatre in 1795 he already had a reputation as an excellent pianist. Born in Bonn, he moved to Vienna aged 22 to receive tuition from Joseph Haydn and, briefly, Mozart. In 1805 his opera *Fidelio* premiered at the Theater an der Wien (see p116).

Gilded statue of Johann Strauss

6 Johann Strauss

Vienna's "Waltz King" (1825–99) was the most successful of a dynasty of composers and musicians. He wrote more than 500 dance pieces, among them the *Blue Danube Waltz* (1876), which became Austria's unofficial national anthem. Strauss is buried at the Zentralfriedhof (see p127).

7 Johannes Brahms
Born in Hamburg in 1833, Brahms became the musical director of the Vienna Singakademie, a choral society, in 1862. For three seasons he directed the Vienna Philharmonic Orchestra, but from 1878 onwards he devoted all of his time to composition. Brahms died in 1897 and is also buried at the Zentralfriedhof.

8 Gustav Mahler
Better known as a conductor, Mahler (1860–1911) also composed ten symphonies and song cycles during his life. He was the musical director of the Staatsoper (1897–1907) and led the opera into its golden age.

Photograph of Gustav Mahler

9 Arnold Schönberg
Founder of the 12-tone serial technique, Schönberg (1874–1951) became one of the 20th century's most renowned composers. He left Vienna in 1933 in the wake of National Socialism and died in the US.

10 Alban Berg
Known for his operas *Wozzeck* (1925) and the unfinished *Lulu*, Berg (1885–1935) suffered under the National Socialist regime, when his music was considered indecent and banned from public stages.

TOP 10 MOZART'S VIENNA

1 Mozarthaus Vienna
Mozart wrote his most famous opera, *The Marriage of Figaro*, here (see p56).

2 Tiefer Graben
MAP M2
Mozart stayed at the house at No. 18 on this street during his first concert tour to Vienna in 1762.

3 Palais Collalto
MAP M2 ▪ Am Hof 13
The six-year-old Mozart gave his first Vienna concert here in 1762.

4 Griechenbeisl
MAP P2 ▪ Fleischmarkt 11
On one of the walls in Vienna's oldest inn you will find Mozart's signature among those of other famous visitors.

5 Stephansdom
Mozart married Constanze Weber on 4 August 1782 in Vienna's impressive cathedral (see pp12–15).

6 Café Frauenhuber
MAP N4 ▪ Himmelpfortgasse 6
Mozart gave piano concerts in the music room of the café.

7 Mozart's Piano
MAP L4 ▪ Neue Burg ▪ Open 10am–6pm Wed–Sun ▪ Adm
Mozart's instrument is housed in the Sammlung alter Musikinstrumente.

8 Mozart's Grave
Mozart was buried at St Marx Cemetery but the site of his actual grave remains unknown (see p130).

9 Mozart Cenotaph
Simmeringer Hauptstrasse ▪ Tram 71
A cenotaph commemorating Mozart was relocated from St Marx Cemetery to the Zentralfriedhof in 1891.

10 Mozartplatz
MAP F4
Characters from the opera *The Magic Flute* watch over the square.

Mozarthaus façade

🔟 Parks and Gardens

① Stadtpark
MAP P5 ■ Parkring

This park, bisected by the River Wien, was designed as an artificial landscape within the city in 1862, with paths winding through grassy areas, past ponds and beautiful shrubs and flowers. But Stadtpark is most famous for the monument to the "King of Waltz", Johann Strauss (see p52).

② Augarten
MAP A5 ■ Obere Augartenstrasse 1

Vienna's oldest park has been open to the public since 1775. Sadly it is now overlooked by the massive anti-aircraft tower built by Hitler's army. However, the formal garden hosts various cultural events during the summer months.

③ Burggarten
MAP L5 ■ Josefsplatz 1

Just behind the National Library is the pretty Burggarten, landscaped in the formal English style and usually inhabited by sun-worshippers on summer days. Located in the large Art Nouveau greenhouse, built in 1901, is a stylish café and restaurant.

④ Schönbrunn Park
The beautiful grounds of the Schloss Schönbrunn include ponds, fountains and a maze (see pp42–5).

Stunning Schönbrunn Park

The Volksgarten in full bloom

⑤ Volksgarten
MAP K3

This garden, between the Burgtheater and Heldenplatz, is popular with students from the nearby university and office workers on their lunch breaks. Its beautiful rose beds bloom spectacularly in spring. The replica of the Temple of Theseus in Athens is used for a range of changing exhibitions.

⑥ Prater
U-Bahn U1 Praterstern

A former 18th-century imperial hunting ground, the Wurstelprater – known as the Prater – is a large public park today. In 2016 it celebrated 250 years of public access. Leafy walks, fairground rides, food stalls, a Ferris wheel and two racecourses are just some of its highlights.

7 Alpengarten im Belvedere

Established in 1803 by the Habsburg Archduke Johann, this is Europe's oldest alpine garden and is part of the Belvedere park (see pp28–9). The beautifully laid out garden is home to more than 4,000 plants, among them an Oriental bonsai collection.

8 Rathauspark
MAP K2

The park in front of the town hall is busy year round with various festivals, ranging from a Christmas market and ice rink in winter to a summer film and music festival. Many monuments and fountains complement the layout of the park. Another attraction is the large number of centuries-old trees.

9 Tiroler Garten
Schloss Schönbrunn ▪ U-Bahn U4

Archduke Johann so admired the Tyrolean landscape and architecture that he ordered that an area within Schönbrunn Park be kept as a natural alpine landscape in the 19th century. Today it boasts an alpine-style house with a small farm and an orchard.

10 Sigmund Freud Park

The green area stretching from Vienna University to the Votivkirche is usually packed with students and picnickers on warm summer days. In the park, a ring of different trees surrounding a granite table and chairs represents the member states of the European Union (see p104).

TOP 10 FOUNTAINS

The Donnerbrunnen fountain

1 Donnerbrunnen
This fountain, created by Georg Raphael Donner in 1737–9, features allegories of Austrian rivers (see p92).

2 Neptunbrunnen
Neptune overlooks cascades at Schönbrunn Palace (see pp42–5).

3 Hochstrahlbrunnen
MAP F5 ▪ Schwarzenbergplatz
The enormous fountain, floodlit on summer nights, was built in 1873.

4 Vermählungsbrunnen
MAP N2 ▪ Hoher Markt
Josef Emanuel von Erlach built this fountain of marble and bronze in 1732.

5 Andromedabrunnen
MAP M2 ▪ Old Town Hall, Wipplingerstrasse 8
The fountain shows princess Andromeda in the fangs of a sea monster, sculpted by Georg Raphael Donner in 1741.

6 Pallas Athene Brunnen
MAP K3 ▪ Dr-Karl-Renner-Ring 3
A statue of the Greek goddess of wisdom towers over the fountain.

7 Danubius Brunnen
MAP M5 ▪ Albertinaplatz
Part of the Albertina building, the fountain features stories of the Danube.

8 Michaelerplatz Brunnen
MAP L3
The monumental fountains of the Hofburg, Macht zu Lande and Macht zur See, can be seen at this square.

9 Schutzengelbrunnen
MAP F4 ▪ Rilkeplatz
Little dragons spout water beneath the angel who gives this fountain its name.

10 Yunus Emre Fountain
Türkenschanzpark ▪ Tram 41
A gift from the Turkish government, the fountain is decorated in gilt script and beautiful tiles.

TOP 10 Underground Vienna

The Third Man sewer tour

1 Sewers

3. Mann Tour: MAP M6; Karlsplatz-Girardipark (U1, U2, U4), opposite the Café Museum; tours May–Oct: 10am–8pm Thu–Sun on the hour; adm; www.drittemanntour.at

Vienna's sewers came to fame in the 1949 film classic *The Third Man*, when Harry Lime, played by Orson Welles, was chased through the city's underworld by the police. Filmed in the rubble of postwar Vienna during the Allied occupation, the movie is still remembered today, as several tours follow in the characters' footsteps.

2 Roman Ruins

MAP N2 ■ Hoher Markt 3 ■ Open 9am–6pm Tue–Sun ■ Adm

Remains of the Roman camp Vindobona (see p48) can be seen at this interesting underground museum. Excavations show archaeological finds such as pottery and coins.

Vindobona remains, outside the Hofburg palace, Michaelerplatz

3 Michaelerkirche Crypt

Well-preserved mummies, some still wearing Baroque frocks and wigs, are preserved in this crypt. From 1631 to 1784, some 4,000 bodies were buried here, including nobles who wanted to rest close to the emperor at Hofburg (see p55).

4 Vienna Art Cult Centre Schottenstift

The Scots' Abbey (see p59) on Freyung has widespread vaults that were continually expanded after its foundation in 1155. The various storage rooms and wine cellars bear remains from the Romanesque, Baroque and Biedermeier periods. Today the area is also used as an exhibition space of the Art Cult Centre.

5 Stephansdom Catacombs

In the 18th century many graveyards across Europe were closed down as plague epidemics spread quickly in the densely populated cities. Some cemeteries were relocated beneath city churches, and people's bones were disinterred and reburied in the crypts. The catacombs underneath the Gothic marvel of Stephansdom were constructed after Emperor Charles VI issued a decree to close the cathedral's graveyard in 1732. They are filled with the bones of some 11,000 people. Today it is hard to imagine that the Stephansplatz was once crammed with gravestones (see p13).

6 Virgilkapelle

MAP N3 ■ Stephansplatz U-Bahn station ■ Open 10am–6pm Tue–Sun & public hols ■ Adm ■ www.wien museum.at

The large Gothic St Virgil's Chapel was only discovered in the 1970s, when the metro line U1 was built – it had been hidden underground for some 200 years. Built in 1250, it was used for public burials until a Vienna merchant turned it into his private crypt in the 14th century.

7 Cabaret Fledermaus

MAP M4 ■ Spiegelgasse 2 ■ Open 9pm–6am Wed–Mon ■ Adm

A long staircase leads down to the Cabaret Fledermaus, named for the bats (Fledermäuse) that inhabited Vienna's cellars in the Middle Ages. The venue plays retro music, but there are also themed nights featuring other genres, some with free admission.

8 Augustinerkirche

MAP M4 ■ Augustinerstrasse 3 (entrance on Josefsplatz) ■ Open 8am–6pm daily ■ Adm

St Augustin's Church was built in 1327 in Gothic style. In the course of its history, many imperial weddings took place here, but the church is most famous for its Herzerlgruft (hearts' crypt) containing the hearts of Austria's emperors.

9 Wine Cellars

In the Middle Ages most Vienna houses had as many storeys below ground as they had above. The cellars stored wine, vegetables and other goods. This underground labyrinth was often connected by tunnels. Many cellars were destroyed during the building of the metro system, but some still exist today as "Keller" (cellar) restaurants. These include the Rathauskeller at Wipplingerstrasse 8 and the Esterhazykeller at Haarhof 1.

Habsburg tomb, Kapuzinergruft crypt

10 Kapuzinergruft

MAP M4 ■ Tegetthoffstrasse 2 ■ Open 10am–6pm daily ■ Adm

The crypt that lies underneath the Kapuzinerkirche (Capuchin Church) was established by Empress Anna in 1618 and served as the burial place of the Habsburg family for over 350 years. Among the 146 elite bodies resting here in elaborately decorated sarcophagi or simple coffins are 12 emperors and 19 empresses. However, their hearts were removed and buried separately in silver containers in the crypt of Augustinerkirche and their intestines in copper urns in the gruesome catacombs of Stephansdom.

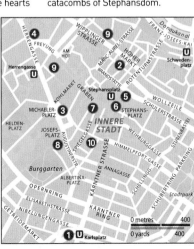

🔟 Off the Beaten Track

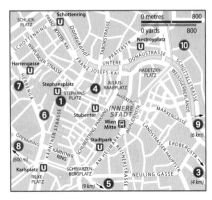

1 Stock im Eisen
MAP N3 ■ **Corner of Graben and Kärntner Strasse, Stephansplatz**
In the Middles Ages, trees were studded with nails for good luck – nails were valuable and the tree an offering to God. A 600-year-old section of such a tree is displayed behind glass on the corner of the striking Palais Equitable mansion.

2 Shopping with Lucie
0680 214 40 74 ■ **www.shoppingwithlucie.com**
Get off the main shopping streets and follow American guide Lucie into designer dens and hidden shops on

Stunning interior of the Jesuit Church

one of her themed three-hour tours, with guaranteed discounts. The tours cost €35.

3 Gasometer
Guglgasse 8
■ **U-Bahn U3** ■ **www.wiener-gasometer.at**
The four large circular Gasometer buildings in Vienna once contained massive amounts of depressurizing gas. Obsolete since 1984, these round silo towers were transformed at the turn of this century into award-winning housing communities and shops *(see p83)*. The whole complex is a fascinating social and eco-project and there are guided tours year-round by arrangement.

4 Jesuitenkirche
For a strange optical illusion, pay a visit to Vienna's Jesuit Church, located in the middle of the old town. The locals swear that there's a cow wearing glasses and playing backgammon in one of the building's 500-year-old murals, but will you be able to spot it? It may be an enlarged version of the kind of humorous marginalia often found in medieval manuscripts *(see p54)*.

Exhibits at the Bestattungsmuseum

8 Damage Unlimited
MAP G3 ▪ Mariahilfer Strasse 23–25 ▪ 0676 668 18 61 ▪ Open 11am–7pm Mon–Sat ▪ www.damage-town.com

Considered Vienna's answer to Comic-Con, Damage Unlimited is where you can play old-fashioned board games or electronic first-person shooters. Look out for the cosplay (costume play) crowd.

5 Bestattungsmuseum
Simmeringer Hauptstrasse 234 ▪ Bus 106 ▪ 01 760 67 ▪ Open 9am–4:30pm Mon–Fri; Mar–Nov: also 10am–5:30pm Sat ▪ www.bestattungsmuseum.at

This unusual museum is testament to a proud Viennese funeral tradition. Housed in Europe's second-largest cemetery, it contains a macabre collection of coffins, pall-bearers' attire, skulls and other oddities that celebrate the business of death.

9 Summer Beaches
Open May–Sep daily

Few visitors know that Vienna has a fine collection of beaches. For some downtime on the city's manmade sandbanks simply bring a picnic, sunscreen and a swimsuit to one of the half a dozen different venues along the Donaukanal.

6 Elmayer Dance School
MAP M3 ▪ Bräunerstrasse 13 ▪ 01 512 71 97 ▪ Lessons 8am–10pm daily ▪ Adm ▪ www.elmayer.at/en

If you have ever fancied mastering the classic Viennese waltz look no further than the Elmayer Dance School, where you can book yourself a lesson. You'll soon be swirling around at 180 beats per minute after 50 minutes of professional tuition with the TV-judge owner from Austria's *Dancing with the Stars*.

Relaxing on one of Vienna's beaches

7 Globe Museum
MAP L2 ▪ Austrian National Library, Herrengasse 9 ▪ 01 534 10 710 ▪ Open 10am–6pm Tue–Sun ▪ Adm ▪ www.onb.ac.at

One of the most fascinating collections of worldly exhibits in Vienna is the Globe Museum – said to be the only museum in the world singularly devoted to globes. Marvel at more than 600 terrestrial and celestial globular maps – some as large as a fully grown man.

10 Republic of Kugelmugel
Antifaschismusplatz 2, Wiener Prater ▪ U-Bahn U2

No need for a passport to visit the Republic of Kugelmugel as this self-proclaimed sovereign micronation is an unusual ball-shaped house located in Prater park. The house was built by Austrian artist Edwin Lipburger in 1971 and the Republic status declared in 1976 after Lipburger fell out with the authorities over building permits. He even printed his own stamps.

📥 Children's Attractions

Exhibit of a scene from the marionette version of Mozart's *The Magic Flute*

① Marionettentheater Schönbrunn

Hofratstrakt, Schloss Schönbrunn
■ U-Bahn Schönbrunn ■ 01 817 32
47 ■ Adm ■ www.marionetten
theater.at

The puppet theatre in the little court theatre at Schönbrunn stages wonderful shows that delight children and adults alike. A version of Mozart's *The Magic Flute* is the undisputed highlight of the programme, with a feather-clad Tamino and a fantastic vicious snake.

Children at the Technisches Museum

② Technisches Museum Wien

An adventure area at this museum is geared towards children aged three to six years old (although older kids enjoy it too) and allows young visitors to experience the natural sciences with hands-on displays. Special, free-of-charge workshops in the museum's kindergarten take place between 1pm and 6pm on Tuesdays, Fridays and Saturdays, as well as from 10am to 6pm on Sundays. This is a great museum for inquisitive little minds (*see p56*).

③ Haus des Meeres

MAP F2 ■ Esterhazypark
■ Open 9am–6pm daily (until 9pm Thu) ■ Adm ■ www.haus-des-meeres.at

Fish and reptiles from all across the world have found a home in a former anti-aircraft tower in Esterhazypark. You can "journey" from the chilly North Sea to the Australian Great Barrier Reef, taking in the natural landscape en route. Very popular with kids are the sharks' and piranhas' feeding time in the "Amazon pool".

④ Adventure Swimming Pool Diana-Tropicana

MAP P1 ■ Lilienbrunngasse 7–9
■ Open 10am–10pm Mon–Sat & public hols, 9am–8pm Sun ■ Adm

There are several adventure pools in Vienna, but the Diana-Tropicana is the only one that features dinosaurs and pirate ships. A water slide that also goes upwards is great fun, too.

5 Schloss Schönbrunn

Young visitors are shown imperial life in the palace from a child's perspective at the Children's Museum. In the Court Bakery they can watch confectioners make cakes and pastries – which can be sampled fresh from the oven (see pp42–5).

6 Schönbrunn Zoo

Considered the oldest zoo in the world, this has all the usual favourites, including elephants, reptiles and butterflies. Most are housed in Baroque-style compounds (see p45).

7 Schmetterlinghaus

MAP L5 ■ Burggarten, Burgring ■ Open Apr–Oct: 10am–4:45pm Mon–Fri, 10am–6:15pm Sat, Sun & public hols; Nov–Mar: 10am–3:45pm daily ■ Adm ■ www.schmetterlinghaus.at

This large Art Nouveau greenhouse contains more than 150 species of tropical butterflies and moths, living in habitats that replicate their natural environment.

8 Schönbrunn Park

This beautiful park is home to two special attractions – the maze and the labyrinth in the palace's gardens. The maze is based on the original 18th-century designs and, once you have made your way through the hedges to the middle, there is a viewing platform over the area. The labyrinth is a games area with a giant kaleidoscope, a climbing pole and fun riddles to solve (see p45).

9 Riesenrad

Prater 90 ■ U-Bahn Praterstern ■ Open Jan, Feb, Nov & Dec: 10am–7:45pm daily; Mar, Apr & Oct: 10am–9:45pm daily; May–Sep: 9am–11:45pm daily ■ Adm ■ www.wiener riesenrad.com

Over 100 years old, Vienna's giant Ferris wheel offers fantastic views over the city's rooftops. Don't miss the small museum in the entrance area, where the history of the wheel and the city are told in some of the Riesenrad's old red cabins.

Getting creative at ZOOM

10 ZOOM

Designed exclusively for children, ZOOM is a place of playful enquiry, learning and discovery. Hands-on exhibitions for toddlers, kitchens for cooking experiments and the chance to "zoom" in on new situations and learn about the world are just some of the highlights at this interactive museum. Booking ahead is recommended (see p35).

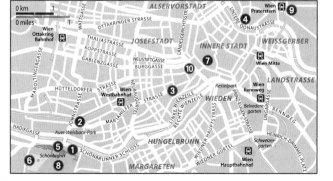

🔟 Theatres

The Volkstheater's sumptuous interior

① Volkstheater

Whereas the Burg, being the Court Theatre, has always been the main stage for classical drama in Vienna, the Volkstheater, or People's Theatre, has always aimed at making modern and classic literature accessible to a broader audience since it was founded in 1889. With nearly 1,000 seats, this is among the largest theatres in the German-speaking world *(see p107)*.

② Rabenhof
Rabengasse 3 ▪ U-Bahn U3
▪ **www.rabenhoftheater.com**

The Rabenhof was constructed as council housing for workers in the 1920s, and an assembly hall for the workers' union was built in the basement. This was adapted to become a theatre between 1987 and 1992. Today the theatre has a colourful programme of modern plays, comedies and other performances on offer.

③ Akademietheater
MAP P6 ▪ Lisztstrasse 1

The Akademietheater is part of the Konzerthaus building *(see p73)*. Initially it functioned as the training stage for the nearby Academy of Music and Performing Arts, but in 1922 it became the "small" venue for the Burgtheater ensemble. Mainly classic modern plays are staged here.

④ Kasino am Schwarzenbergplatz
MAP F5 ▪ Schwarzenbergplatz 1

This is a small and intimate stage, located in a former officers' mess of the imperial army that was adapted as a venue in the 1990s. Its extensive programme includes contemporary plays, often followed by talks with the actors.

⑤ Raimundtheater
Wallgasse 18–20 ▪ U-Bahn U6

The theatre is named after Austrian actor and playwright Ferdinand Raimund (1790–1836), as it opened with one of his plays in 1893. The Raimundtheater has always specialized in music – after a period of staging operettas, today it is mainly used as a venue for musicals.

Performance at the Raimundtheater

⑥ Theater in der Josefstadt
MAP D2 ▪ Josefstädter Strasse 26 ▪ www.josefstadt.org

Built in 1788 following the design of Josef Kornhäusel, this theatre was entirely rebuilt in 1822 and reopened with a musical piece by Beethoven, composed for the occasion.

7 Kammerspiele
MAP P2

■ Rotenturmstrasse 20

This 515-seat theatre was built in 1910 and fully refurbished in 2013. First known as the Residenztheater, it is closely connected to the Theater in der Josefstadt and actors usually perform in different plays in both venues. The Kammerspiele's programme is made up entirely of comedies.

8 Vienna's English Theatre
MAP D2 ■ Josefsgasse 12 ■ www.englishtheatre.at

Vienna's English Theatre was founded in 1963 and is the oldest English-language theatre in continental Europe. It was initially intended as a summer venue for tourists but soon extended its programme to run all year round. The stage has attracted world stars such as Anthony Quinn and Judi Dench to its successful productions.

9 Schauspielhaus
MAP B3 ■ Porzellangasse 19 ■ www.schauspielhaus.at

The Schauspielhaus is a venue that offers a multifaceted programme, including literary readings and light operas as well as contemporary drama. Since its foundation in 1978,

the theatre has seen not only many Austrian but also several world premieres, particularly by the Hungarian-born dramatist George Tabori (1914–2007). It is also one of the many venues for productions staged by the Wiener Festwochen, Vienna's most important theatre festival (see p86). Being fairly small, the audience has the advantage of being very close to the actors during the performances.

10 Burgtheater
The Burgtheater, or the imperial Court Theatre, is one of the most important theatres in the German-speaking world, and the choice of its director at any given period always arouses much political and cultural passion. Premieres of traditional as well as modern plays are closely scrutinized by the public, triggering either enthusiastic or dismissive reactions (see p93).

Vienna's Burgtheater

🔟 Music Venues

Gala concert performance at Vienna's Musikverein

① Theater an der Wien

Having been a musical venue for many years, this stunning historic theatre is once again a working opera house *(see p116)*.

② Ronacher

MAP N4 ▪ Seilerstätte 9 ▪ www.musicalvienna.at

The original Ronacher, built in 1870, staged tragedies and comedies, but after it burned down in the 1880s architects Ferdinand Fellner and Hermann Helmer replaced it with a variety theatre. Neglected after World War II, the Ronacher reopened in 1988 with the musical *Cats*.

③ Musikverein

Public concert life began in Vienna with the foundation of the Society of Friends of Music in 1812; up until then, concerts were restricted to aristocratic homes. This grand concert hall *(see p121)* was commissioned by the society in 1869 after previous locations had become too small. The society's aim was, and still is, to promote all music; until 1909 it also ran a music academy with teachers such as Anton Bruckner and eminent students such as Gustav Mahler *(see p61)*. The school was the predecessor of the present Academy of Music.

④ RadioKulturhaus

MAP G5 ▪ Argentinierstrasse 30a ▪ www.radiokulturhaus.orf.at

The RadioKulturhaus offers a programme of jazz and classical concerts, literary readings and films. Most of the concerts are broadcast on the radio station Ö1.

⑤ Porgy & Bess

MAP P4 ▪ Riemergasse 11 ▪ www.porgy.at

One of the top jazz clubs in town is mainly dedicated to modern jazz. Alongside star names, many newcomers also get the chance to play.

Façade of the Ronacher theatre

6 Jazzland

MAP P2 ■ Franz-Josefs-Kai 29 ■ www.jazzland.at

This traditional jazz club, founded in 1972, has a history of distinguished international and national artists performing in its cellar venue.

7 Volksoper
MAP A2 ■ Währinger Strasse 78 ■ www.volksoper.at

The "People's Opera" opened in 1898 after a group of industrialists raised funds to celebrate Franz Joseph's Golden Jubilee. The theatre's façade has remained unchanged. Operettas and dances are performed here.

8 Staatsoper
In a city so intrinsically linked to classical music, no visitor should miss a tour of the spectacular State Opera House (see pp36–7).

Interior of the Staatsoper

9 Kammeroper
MAP P2 ■ Fleischmarkt 24 ■ www.theater-wien.at

The Kammeroper, founded in 1954, is dedicated to promoting young singers. The five main productions a year include classic and Baroque operas, as well as some contemporary works.

10 Konzerthaus
MAP P6 ■ Lothringerstrasse 20 www.konzerthaus.at

The Vienna Concert House opened in 1913. Its design, by Ferdinand Fellner and Hermann Helmer, is clearly influenced by Art Nouveau style. With four concert halls, more than 3,100 seats, and a diverse programme, the venue attracts music lovers from all camps.

TOP 10 NIGHTCLUBS

Inside the Volksgarten nightclub

1 Volksgarten
Everything from tango to R&B nights is on offer here (see p95).

2 B72
U-Bahnbogen 72–3 ■ U-Bahn U6
This trendy club in the arcades of the U6 metro plays electronic music.

3 U4
Schönbrunner Strasse 222 ■ U-Bahn U4
Next to the U4 stop, this place hosts theme nights from boogie to classic rock.

4 Eden Bar
MAP N4 ■ Liliengasse 2
This tiny cellar bar is a popular meeting point for Vienna's high society.

5 Rhiz
U-Bahnbögen 37–8 ■ U-Bahn U6
Also in the arcades of the metro, Rhiz has a daily DJ line-up of electronic music.

6 Flex
MAP B4 ■ Augartenbrücke
This underground club next to the river has a lively indie scene.

7 Chelsea
Lerchenfelder Gürtel, U-Bahnbögen 29–30 ■ U-Bahn U6
Live bands and indie music under the U6 metro line.

8 Escalera
MAP A2 ■ U-Bahn U6 ■ Stadtbahnbögen 181–182
Classy dance venue, so dress to impress.

9 Arena
Baumgasse 80 ■ Bus 77A
Music here ranges from punk to indie.

10 Titanic
MAP F3 ■ U-Bahn U3 ■ Theobaldgasse 11
Spread over two floors, the music here is old-style disco.

Viennese Dishes

1 Zwiebelrostbraten
Slices of roast beef are topped with fried onion rings and served with mashed or roasted potatoes. A variation is *vanillerostbraten*, in which the meat is seasoned with garlic.

2 Leberknödelsuppe
Austrians are fond of their soups and a traditional three-course Sunday lunch will often start off with a bowl of clear beef broth. This particular variety, with little liver dumplings, is undoubtedly the king among Austrian soups.

3 Frankfurters
The takeaway sausage stall, or *würstelstand*, is found all over Vienna. Slim, pale sausages were introduced to Vienna in 1798 by the butcher Johann Georg Lahner, who named them after the city of Frankfurt, where they originated. They are usually served with mustard and a *semmel* (bread roll).

Tafelspitz, Franz Joseph's favourite

5 Tafelspitz
Meat is essential to Viennese cuisine, and beef has played an important role throughout the centuries. The favourite among the many variations is boiled rump, usually served with *rösti* (fried grated potatoes) or boiled potatoes and apple and horseradish sauce. Emperor Franz Joseph allegedly ate *tafelspitz* every single day.

Tasty breaded Weiner schnitzel

6 Wiener Schnitzel
The roots of the *Wiener schnitzel* lie in ancient Byzantium, where meat was purportedly eaten after being sprinkled with gold. Over the course of time the precious metal was replaced by a coat of golden breadcrumbs. Count Radetzky, who fought several wars for the Austrian Empire in the 19th century, is said to have brought the dish to imperial Vienna from Milan. The outcome is tasty veal or pork covered in breadcrumbs and fried until golden. The classic side dish is potato salad.

4 Frittatensuppe
Most soups are made of clear beef stock and are served with a range of garnishes to create some variety. Adding *frittaten* – pancakes seasoned with a sprinkle of fresh herbs, cut into thin strips and served in bouillon – is a popular option.

7 Schweinsbraten mit Semmelknödel
Roast pork is another standard of Viennese cuisine. It is variously seasoned with flavours ranging from garlic to fresh herbs and caraway, and the meat is generally served with dumplings, salad and gravy.

A bowl of Frittatensuppe

8 Gefüllte Paprika

Stuffed peppers are a remnant of the Austro-Hungarian monarchy, when Vienna was quite a melting pot. Originally from the Balkans, the dish soon became popular throughout the city. Green peppers are stuffed with minced meat and rice and usually served with a tomato sauce.

9 Knödel

Vienna's many dumpling types, both sweet and savoury, include plain *knödel* with vegetables and meat, *germknödel* (dumplings with sour prune jam), *zwetschgenknödel* (plum dumplings), *topfenknödel* (curd cheese dumpling) and *griessnockerl* (semolina dumplings).

***Zwetschgenknödel* (plum dumplings)**

10 Gulasch

This dish is a successful marriage of Austrian and Hungarian cuisines. The original Hungarian soup-like dish arrived in Viennese kitchens and evolved into goulash – a spicy beef stew, seasoned with paprika and served with dumplings or bread rolls. It can also come with potatoes or a fried egg and gherkins.

Beef *Gulasch*

TOP 10 VIENNESE CAKES

Classic *Schwarzwälderkirschtorte*

1 Schwarzwälderkirschtorte
Black Forest Gateau is a rich chocolate cake with layers of sponge sandwiched together with cream and sour cherries.

2 Gugelhupf
With almonds, cocoa or chocolate icing, this cake is baked in a fluted ring mould and is named for its shape.

3 Apfelstrudel
Strudel is an Austrian staple. Very thin dough is sprinkled with apples, cinnamon, raisins and icing sugar.

4 Dobostorte
This cake features eight layers of light sponge joined together with chocolate cream and glazed on top with caramel.

5 Linzertorte
Named after the Austrian city of Linz, this almond pastry filled with jam has been popular for nearly 300 years.

6 Malakofftorte
Cream and sponge biscuits drenched in rum are set together and smothered in butter-cream icing.

7 Esterhazytorte
This cake is made with almond sponge layers filled with cream and covered with marbled brown-and-white icing.

8 Rehrücken
This chocolate cake is shaped like a saddle of deer, although no one now knows the origin of this. The sponge is usually filled with apricot jam.

9 Sachertorte
Franz Sacher allegedly invented this rich cake, covered with apricot jam then coated with chocolate, in 1832.

10 Cremeschnitte
This consists of two layers of crispy puff pastry filled with a thick layer of vanilla-flavoured whipped cream.

📻🔟 Restaurants

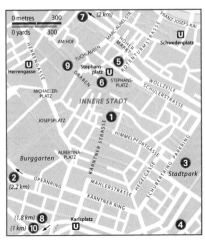

2 Die Wäscherei

Although this restaurant is not on anyone's list of the best fine-dining establishments, there's no better place for brunch in the city. Vienna's young residents flock here for its €16 all-you-can-eat menu. Set in an old laundry, Die Wäscherei serves vegetarian, Indian, Israeli and Spanish fare, alongside Viennese comfort food (see p111).

3 Steirereck

With its fabulous service, culinary artistry and location in Vienna's Stadtpark, this is arguably the best restaurant in the city. Under the guidance of chef Heinz Reitbauer, its menus exhibit stunning flair and have both regional and international influences. The specialities include sturgeon fillets in pepper sauce with crispy olives, and the freshwater mountain fish, char, which is cooked at the table in hot beeswax. Its cellar holds around 25,000 bottles of international and Austrian wines. It's best to book ahead (see p99).

1 Restaurant im Hotel Ambassador

Located on the first floor of the Hotel Ambassador, this gourmet restaurant offers traditional Austrian cuisine with contemporary touches. Seasonal dishes, such as venison and wild boar, feature on the menu, as well as fish and vegetarian fare. The modern dining room is pleasantly light and spacious, overlooking the Neuer Markt. Reservations are essential (see p99).

Modern interior of Steirereck, one of the best restaurants in Vienna

Inside the elegant Weinzirl

4 Weinzirl
A marriage of music and food, the Weinzirl is the in-house restaurant of the Konzerthaus, with an award-winning emphasis on cutting-edge contemporary cooking, in a clean modern dining room *(see p99)*.

5 Wrenkh
In a city of meat-eaters, Wrenkh is a salad bowl of rucola, mushrooms, papaya and quinoa. The young Wrenkh brothers also preside over a renowned vegetarian cooking school. Wrenkh is no longer Vienna's only vegan or vegetarian eatery, but it remains the most popular *(see p99)*.

6 DO & CO Stephansplatz
If you enjoy a restaurant with a comfortable atmosphere and international cuisine, then this small but elegant bistro is the place for you. It is particularly popular for lunch or early dinner, but many people come just to read the newspapers and enjoy a coffee. In winter, oysters are a speciality *(see p99)*.

7 Kim
Arguably Austria's most famous female chef, Sohyi Kim has set up a restaurant in a tiny new location – with only ten seats. A prolific writer, with her own Kim Chi product line, Kim has become an institution in her adopted city of Vienna. Her "5 elements" fusion dishes are personally prepared in surprise menus. Credit card reservations are mandatory *(see p105)*.

8 Steman
This eatery is the epitome of old-fashioned and inexpensive traditional cooking. A typical Viennese tavern with bright green fridges and a dining room with white tablecloths and parquet floors, it may be overlooked by gourmet magazines, but is always packed with punters to the high white ceilings every weekday. The *Wiener schnitzel* and goulash are to die for. Reservations are a must *(see p119)*.

9 Meinl am Graben
There is nobody in Vienna who has not eaten here. Set above the Meinl grocery emporium is an elegant, quiet gourmet dining room, with an exceptional wine list and seats looking down on the busy Graben high street. Dishes are traditional, and desserts are delicious. Breakfast, lunch, high tea and evening meals attract loyal devotees. The restaurant is rated as one of the very best in the city each year *(see p99)*.

Seasonal dishes at Meinl am Graben

10 Zu den drei Buchteln
Neither the decor nor the cuisine has changed since 1950 in this temple to Bohemian classic dishes. Specialities include the eponymous *buchteln* yeast cakes. Cooked by two charming Czech ladies, the food is authentic and portions ample. This is not the place to go if you are looking for nouvelle cuisine *(see p119)*.

For a key to restaurant price ranges see p99

🔟 Cafés

1 Café Demel

This café, part of which resembles a Rococo-period salon, is Vienna's most refined retreat for cake lovers. Opened in 1786, it had become a hot spot for the Viennese upper classes by the mid-19th century, even providing the beloved Empress Sisi with her favourite sweet violet sorbet (see p98).

2 Café Museum

Designed by the minimalist architect Adolf Loos in 1899, this café reflects his anti-ornamental aesthetic. Remodelled in the 1930s, it has since been returned to Loos's original design (see p118).

3 Café Diglas

Established in 1923, the Diglas has marble tables, wooden chairs and little window booths fitted with red velvet sofas. Ordering a piece of cake – slices are served with a small mountain of whipped cream – is highly recommended (see p98).

4 Café Europa

This café has all the amenities of a traditional coffee house, but with modern plastic chairs and a cheerful informality. It is famous for being open until 5am, providing both pastries and cooked meals of Viennese comfort food around the clock. There's also an American-style cocktail bar (see p118).

Graceful façade of Café Landtmann

5 Café Landtmann

Franz Landtmann opened his café in 1873. Sigmund Freud used to have his morning coffee here, as did the artistic director of the Burgtheater, Max Reinhardt. Landtmann bustles with activity day and night – it has a large shaded terrace, and the four interior rooms are elegantly decorated with velvet upholstery, starched linen tablecloths, crystal light fixtures and large mirrors with inlaid wood (see p98).

6 Café Central

One of the city's best-known cafés, the Central was the meeting place for Vienna's intellectuals at the turn of the 19th century – the poet Peter Altenberg gathered a literary circle and he even had his mail delivered here. Leon Trotsky was also one of the regulars during his Vienna exile prior to World War I. Today the Central serves almost 1,000 cups of coffee a day in its elegant setting (see p98).

Enchanting interior of Café Central

7 Café Bräunerhof
This place has an authentic living-room atmosphere, cosy but worn, thanks to a stream of customers dating back to the 1900s. It has always been a literary café – the writers Alfred Polgar and Hugo von Hofmannsthal were regulars (see p98).

8 Café Hawelka
Bustling Hawelka, opened in the 1930s, has old-world charm. The owners often took paintings from artists in exchange for food – as a result the walls are covered with works by Ernst Fuchs, among others (see p98).

Café Hawelka's poster-covered walls

9 Café Prückel
Famous for its 1950s ambience, this café hosts music and plays in its basement (see p98).

10 Café Sperl
Built in grand style in 1880, Sperl has always been a haunt of artists, singers and musicians from the nearby Theater an der Wien. Concerts take place every Sunday afternoon from September to June (see p118).

TOP 10 TYPES OF COFFEE

Viennese coffees

1 Melange
This is a blend of strong coffee and hot milk, served with foamed milk or whipped cream on the top.

2 Grosser Brauner
A large cup of black coffee is served with a tiny jug of coffee-flavoured cream on the side.

3 Kleiner Brauner
This is the smaller version of the *Grosser Brauner* but is also served with coffee-flavoured cream.

4 Grosser Schwarzer
The drink for real coffee addicts – a very large, strong cup of black coffee with no accompaniment.

5 Kleiner Schwarzer
As the smaller version of the *Grosser Schwarzer*, this is simply a small cup of black coffee.

6 Verlängerter
This is the "lengthened" variety of a *Brauner*, a coffee weakened slightly with hot water and served with milk instead of cream.

7 Kaisermelange
Not to everyone's taste, a *Kaisermelange* is a large black coffee mixed with egg yolk, honey and Cognac.

8 Einspänner
In this famous drink, strong coffee is served in a glass with a crown of whipped cream on top.

9 Fiaker
A large cup of coffee is refined with rum. It is named after the city's famous horse-drawn carriages.

10 Eiskaffee
For this drink, cold coffee is served with vanilla ice cream and whipped cream in a tall glass.

🔟 Heurigen

Pretty Fuhrgassl-Huber *heuriger*

① Fuhrgassl-Huber
Neustift am Walde 68 ▪ Bus 41A ▪ 01 440 14 05 ▪ €€

With seating for 800 people, this busy *heurigen* (see p141), located on the edge of the Vienna Woods (see p128), is one of the city's largest wine taverns. Glasses of the most recent vintage can be accompanied with food from the buffet, which serves everything from smoked ham and cheese to delicious *Wiener schnitzel*.

② Hengl-Haselbrunner
Iglaseegasse 10 ▪ U-Bahn U4, U6 ▪ 01 320 33 30 ▪ €€

Grinzing (see p128) was once a small community of wine-growers, but today it has one of the highest densities of *heurigen* in Vienna. Hengl-Haselbrunner is slightly off the beaten track, but offers excellent red and white wines, as well as a buffet menu of regional specialities.

③ Zimmermann
Mitterwurzergasse 20 ▪ Bus 35A ▪ 01 440 12 07 ▪ Closed Nov–mid-Mar ▪ €

In rural isolation on the edge of the Vienna Woods, Zimmermann has a petting zoo with all sorts of small animals, and there is a great friendly, family atmosphere. Enjoy a glass of the new vintages with dishes from the buffet and, in summer, sit out amid the picturesque Neustift vineyards.

Visitors enjoying the scenery at Sirbu

④ Kierlinger
Kahlenberger Strasse 20 ▪ Train Nussdorf ▪ 01 370 22 64 ▪ No credit cards ▪ €

The white wines of this traditional tavern are counted among Vienna's best – be sure to sample a glass of their Chardonnay or Weissburgunder. Kierlinger is also known for its tasty Liptauer spread, made of cheese with paprika, onions, gherkins and spices. The *heuriger* has a large garden, and cultural events take place in the evening all year round.

⑤ Mayer am Pfarrplatz
Pfarrplatz 2 ▪ U-Bahn U4; bus 38A ▪ 01 370 12 87 ▪ €€

The historic building now occupied by Mayer am Pfarrplatz was once the home of Ludwig van Beethoven (see p60). He spent the summer of 1817 here when he hoped to find relief for his worsening deafness. Today you can soak up the atmosphere and enjoy excellent food and home-produced wines. It's an acclaimed winery and has won many national and international prizes. Viennese music is played every evening.

⑥ Sirbu
Kahlenberger Strasse 210 ▪ Train and taxi Nussdorf ▪ 01 320 59 28 ▪ Closed Sun ▪ €

This *heuriger*, tucked away on Kahlenberg mountain (see p129), has a stunning setting amid vineyards and trees, and is lovely at night. The usual *heurigen* dishes and home-grown wines are served.

7 Zahel

Maurer Hauptplatz 9 ▪ Bus 60A, 56B; tram 60 ▪ 01 889 13 18 (call for openings) ▪ Closed Sun ▪ No credit cards ▪ €

The reds and whites from Zahel, an up-and-coming winery, should not be missed. This *heuriger's* buffet has a varying selection of à la carte dishes.

Terrace seating outside Reinprecht

8 Reinprecht

Cobenzlgasse 22 ▪ U-Bahn U4, U6 ▪ 01 320 14 71 0 ▪ Open Jan–Feb: Fri & Sat; Mar–Dec: daily ▪ €€

Located in a former monastery in Grinzing, Reinprecht has seating in the old vaults as well as on garden terraces. The wines are home grown, music is played every evening and classic *heurigen* food is served.

9 Christ

Amtsstrasse 14 ▪ Bus 32A; Tram 31, 32 ▪ 01 292 51 52 ▪ Open from 3pm daily (odd months only) ▪ €

The Christ family has been producing wine for 400 years, winning many awards. Traditional and cosy with a peaceful garden, this *heurigen* serves seasonal traditional food, such as asparagus, mushroom or game.

10 Wieninger

Stammersdorfer Strasse 31 ▪ Bus 30A ▪ 01 292 41 06 ▪ Closed Mon–Wed ▪ No credit cards ▪ €€

This family business achieves the perfect balance of serving excellent wines with great food. Largely frequented by locals, Wieninger is less expensive than *heurigen* located in the more famous communities of Grinzing and Nussdorf.

TOP 10 DRINKS

1 White Wines
Austria's superb sweet dessert wines are among the world's best. Vienna is the only capital in the world that produces wine. The main varieties are Grüner Veltliner and Weissburgunder.

2 Red Wines
Austria also produces excellent red wines, including Zweigelt, Blauer Portugieser and Blaufränkisch.

3 Gespritzter
Sparkling water mixed with table wine is an all-time favourite in Austria, particularly in summer.

4 Sparkling Wines
The Austrian sparkling wine Sekt is an increasingly popular drink.

5 Beers
Several breweries in Vienna produce very good, malty beers. Restaurants and bars usually offer a *Seidl* (0.33 litre/ 0.7 pt) or a *Krügel* (0.5 litre/1pt).

6 Soft Drinks
Apple juice and grape juice mixed (*gespritzt*) with sparkling water is a popular soft drink in Vienna, as is *Almdudler*, a herbal lemonade.

7 Sturm
For a few short weeks during the autumn, fermenting grape juice is available. Although it tastes sweet, it is alcoholic and quite powerful.

8 Mulled Wines
Around Christmas, hot spicy wine and punch are warming and very popular.

9 Coffee
Vienna's first coffee house opened in 1683; the city's coffee house culture was awarded UNESCO status in 2011.

10 Schnapps
A distilled eau de vie made from fruits such as apricots or juniper berries.

Bottles of schnapps

For a key to restaurant price ranges see p99

TOP 10 Markets, Malls and Department Stores

Luxury goods on display in the Steffl department store

1 Steffl
MAP N4 ■ Kärntner Strasse 19

This major department store is located in the heart of the city. You'll find mainly designer names such as Ralph Lauren and Calvin Klein on its five floors, but there are also perfumes, cosmetic products and home decor items on sale. The top floor has great views over the rooftops and the Sky Bar offers excellent cocktails.

2 Naschmarkt
Unmissable for any visitor interested in busy, colourful markets, the Naschmarkt has everything from fruit and vegetables to a Saturday flea market *(see p116)*.

3 Karmelitermarkt
MAP C5 ■ Im Werd, Krummbaumgasse, Leopoldsgasse & Haidgasse

A daily market takes place on the square encircled by these four streets. It's a bustling spot where you can buy vegetables, fruit, meat and Turkish food, and investigate kosher butchers and grocery shops. At weekends, farmers and vendors come from outside Vienna to set up their tables and sell their produce.

4 Ringstrassen Galerien
MAP M6 ■ Kärntner Strasse/ Kärntner Ring

This elegant shopping centre is Vienna's most expensive retail area, with designer clothes as well as jewellery and gourmet food. The shops are interspersed with cafés and restaurants.

5 Wien Mitte The Mall
MAP R4 ■ Landstrasser Hauptstrasse 1b

This spacious, modern shopping mall is located at Wien Mitte station. You'll find all kinds of goods here, from fashion labels to shoe shops, electronic items to jewellery, as well as a supermarket that is open on Sundays. There are cafés and restaurants aplenty for weary shoppers.

6 Rochusmarkt
MAP R4 ■ Landstrasser Hauptstrasse 51

Just outside the Rochusgasse metro station, this small market has some 30 permanent stalls offering mainly fruit, vegetables, flowers and fresh meat. On Saturdays it doubles in size, when farmers from further afield come to sell their home-grown crops.

7 Am Hof
MAP M2

The Baroque Am Hof square, with its unique architectural surroundings and cobbled streets, is the perfect setting for an antiques market. Vendors offer all kinds of antique goods on Fridays and Saturdays, but the market is best known for its second-hand books – you might be lucky and find a rare or early edition of your favourite title.

8 Gasometer

These four round industrial buildings were constructed in 1899 to store gas. No longer needed for their original purpose, they were converted in 2001 by four renowned architects (Coop Himmelblau, Jean Nouvel, Manfred Wehdorn and Wilhelm Holzbauer) into an events hall, 615 apartments, a students' hall of residence and a shopping centre with around 70 shops offering everything from fashion to electronic goods. The four separate buildings are connected by glazed corridors *(see p66)*.

Browsing Freyung's Easter market

9 Freyung
MAP L2

In medieval times both festivals and executions took place on the Freyung, but it is largely markets that are held here today. It's a real Viennese experience. A farmers' market selling mainly organic produce takes place every two weeks and, just before Christmas, a bustling festive market sells all sorts of handmade art and vendors offer alcoholic punch. It also has a picturesque Easter market.

10 Gerngross
MAP F2 ■ Mariahilfer Strasse 38–48

One of Vienna's largest department stores, Gerngross has goods ranging from designer clothing to middle-of-the-range labels, from fashion accessories to home decor. There is a sushi restaurant and a café on the top floor, both offering an excellent view over the bustling shopping street *(see p117)* down below.

The iconic Gasometer buildings

Vienna for Free

Schloss Schönbrunn gardens

1 Schloss Schönbrunn Gardens

Although entry to Vienna's grandest palace is pricey, visitors can stroll the delightful gardens for free. Schloss Schönbrunn is a horticultural wonder, with sumptuous planting and pretty fountains, and to wander through it is an absolute joy (see pp42–5).

2 Magical Music

Summer nights concert: www. sommernachtskonzert.at ■ Donauinselfest: www.donauinselfest.at ■ Staatsoper concerts: www.wien.info

In June, free open-air concerts include the Vienna Philharmonic in Schloss Schönbrunn gardens and three days of live music at Europe's biggest free party at Donauinsel. A giant screen on Herbert-von-Karajan Platz shows Staatsoper concerts all summer.

Open-air Vienna Philharmonic concert

3 The Hofburg

While many of the dazzling imperial residences of the Hofburg palace charge for entry, the maze of stone passages, Michaelerkirche and Augustinerkirche can be visited for free (see pp16–19).

4 Tours of the Rathaus

Free state room tours of Vienna's Rathaus reveal some of the city's lesser-known political secrets and are rich in controversy, power struggles and mayoral intrigue (see p108).

5 Walking Tour

WomWalk: departs Wombat's, Rechte Wienzeile 35, Naschmarkt; 01 897 23 36; 10:30am Mon, Wed, Fri & Sat; www.wombats-hostels.com

Take advantage of the city's only free walking tour, departing four days a week from the Wombats Hostel in Naschmarkt. It's a great way for solo travellers to make new friends.

6 Danube Dipping

The beach at the tip of the summer party island of Donauinsel in the middle of the Danube river is a designated FKK zone for clothes-optional sun-bathing. FKK stands for *freikörperkultur*, meaning "culture of free bodies". Stripping off in this verdant waterfront setting costs nothing and you can also drink at the bars here *au naturel*.

7 Sankt-Marxer-Freidhof

Take a leisurely stroll around the famous St Marx Cemetery (see p130). Among the 18th-century tombs, burial chambers and carved crosses, you'll spot a gravestone that honours beloved composer Wolfgang Amadeus Mozart (his body is thought to be buried elsewhere in a pauper's grave).

8 Museum Entry
Wien Museum: www.wienmuseum.at

Museums, such as the Museum für angewandte Kunst (MAK), offer free entry to under 19s. Most are free on National Day (26 October). MAK is free from 6pm to 10pm on Tuesday (see p56), and there is free admission on the first Sunday of the month at all Wien Museum sites.

Prater park and its Ferris wheel

9 Prater

It doesn't cost a penny to wander around the Prater, the large public park in the east of the city. So, unless you want to ride the funfair or dine out at the food stalls, the magic, music and mayhem of 200 attractions are all free (see p62).

10 Cinematic Splendour
Various venues ■ Jun–Sep: 9pm daily ■ check www.virtualvienna.net/open-air-cinema for details

Vienna runs an open-air cinema programme during the summer and it's an atmospheric way to catch a movie for free. Simply pack some snacks and bring a blanket for an evening under a star-filled sky.

TOP 10 BUDGET TIPS

Bikes at a CityBike docking station

1 Make use of the free hour's bike hire from CityBike, Vienna's public rental scheme. Register online (see p135) or at one of the 120 docking stations and return the bike to another station within an hour.

2 Don't waste your money on fancy bottled waters as Vienna's high-quality drinking water comes straight from a sparkling mountain lake.

3 Pick up a money-saving Vienna PASS (www.viennapass.com) for free entry to over 60 top attractions, museums and monuments plus discount travel.

4 No need to rack up hefty mobile bills while you're exploring Vienna as free Wi-Fi is available in almost all central public places.

5 Last-minute cut-priced theatre and music tickets are available from venues on the day (www.viennaconcerts.com).

6 Maximize cheap travel by avoiding peak travel times and buying a multiday travel pass for 24, 48 or 72 hours (www.wienerlinien.at).

7 Head to Neubau for the city's best cheap eats. Some places charge only what you can afford to pay.

8 Visit the Saturday flea market (flohmarkt) in the Naschmarkt for some unique shoestring bargains (see p116).

9 For a cheaper alternative to an open-top bus ride take the tram: a scenic option at a fraction of the price (www.wienerlinien.at).

10 To take a self-guided walking tour, download a free map from City Walks (www.city-walks.info/Vienna/).

🔟 Festivals

Colourful painted Easter eggs

1 Easter Markets
Mar/Apr

Austria's Easter tradition is to decorate branches of pussy willow with painted eggshells hung on string. Easter Egg Markets are also held on squares and in front of churches.

2 Wiener Festwochen
May/Jun

Various theatre and dance companies stage productions in this annual festival at venues including the MuseumsQuartier, the Ronacher and Theater an der Wien *(see pp34–5 & 72)*.

3 Jazzfest
Mid-Jun–early Jul

Traditional homes of classical music such as the State Opera and the Konzerthaus turn into jazz venues during Vienna's annual Jazzfest, where you can see world-famous jazz musicians perform all over the city.

4 Oper Klosterneuburg
Jul

This festival stages glamorous performances of opera classics in the courtyard of Klosterneuburg abbey, the palatial religious foundation that dominates the town of the same name just north of Vienna *(see p130)*. There are also fascinating behind-the-scenes workshops for children.

5 Musikfilmfest
Jul–Aug

Every year the square in front of Vienna's Town Hall turns into a bustling hub for music lovers. Every evening crowds flock to watch concerts and opera and operetta performances broadcast on a huge screen. Just as popular are the food stalls where Mexican, Japanese, Greek and Austrian specialities can all be found.

6 ImPulsTanz
Jul–Aug

Vienna turns into the capital of dance when the international dance festival takes place at various theatres.

Dancer performing at ImPulsTanz

7 Viennale
Oct

Vienna's international film festival, the Viennale, features screenings in cinemas in the historic city centre. These include films that would probably not make it to mainstream cinemas in other circumstances. Accompanying debates and events take place in a tent in Stadtpark.

Wien Modern
Late Oct–Nov
Founded by Claudio Abbado in 1988, Wien Modern is one of Europe's few genuinely successful festivals for post-1945 and contemporary "classical" music. The emphasis is on the avant-garde, and the concerts play to large and enthusiastic audiences.

One of Vienna's Christmas markets

Christmas Markets
Nov–Dec
In the weeks leading up to Christmas you'll find numerous festive markets across Vienna's squares and pedestrianized zones. The stalls sell small gifts and Christmas decorations, as well as punch and hot spiced wine to warm you on cold winter evenings.

Ball Season
Dec–Feb
Viennese life revolves around the waltz, at least between Christmas and Lent, when the calendar is full with evenings of dancing. Balls in the Hofburg palace are the most splendid, but there are dances every evening in many of Vienna's hotels, concert halls and, once a year, in the Staatsoper (see pp36–7).

Guests at the Staatsoper ball

TOP 10 RELIGIOUS FESTIVALS

Christmas mass in Stephansdom

1 Epiphany
6 Jan
Children dress as the Three Wise Men and bring news of Christ's birth.

2 Easter
Mar/Apr
The resurrection of Christ is celebrated with fires and light processions.

3 Christ's Ascension
May/Jun (40 days after Easter)
Celebrated to mark the day that Christ ascended to heaven.

4 Pentecost
May/Jun (50 days after Easter)
Celebrates the Holy Ghost being sent to unite the world's peoples.

5 Corpus Christi
May/Jun (60 days after Easter)
Processions are held and a monstrance is carried from altar to altar.

6 Mary's Ascension
15 Aug
This day commemorates the Virgin Mary's ascension to heaven.

7 All Saints' Day
1 Nov
Austrians visit the graves of their loved ones to light candles and lay wreaths.

8 Mary's Conception
8 Dec
On this day, St Anne conceived a daughter, the Virgin Mary.

9 Christmas Eve
24 Dec
The most important day of the celebrations, as families gather around the Christmas tree and open presents.

10 Christmas Day
25 Dec
A holy day when people attend church and visit their families.

Vienna
Area by Area

Bird's-eye view of Vienna from the
North Tower of Stephansdom

TOP 10 Central Vienna

With cobbled streets, narrow alleys, quiet squares and a wealth of historic buildings, Vienna's atmospheric heart is brimming with famous landmarks and reminders of both Roman and Habsburg rule, yet it also hosts the *crème de la crème* of shops, restaurants and the city's famous cafés and coffee shops. Although the inner city is popular with Vienna's many visitors, nowhere else will you find so many elegant locals proudly promenading as you will along the Kärntner Strasse, Graben and Kohlmarkt – indeed, most of the central area is now pedestrianized.

Art Nouveau Anker Uhr clock by Franz von Matsch

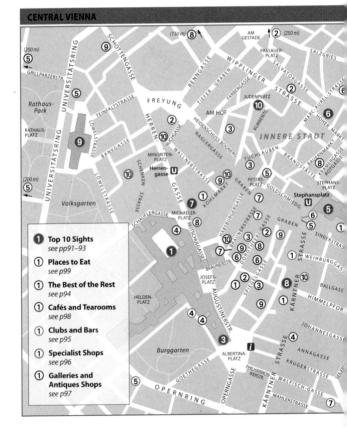

CENTRAL VIENNA

1. **Top 10 Sights**
   see pp91–93
1. **Places to Eat**
   see p99
1. **The Best of the Rest**
   see p94
1. **Cafés and Tearooms**
   see p98
1. **Clubs and Bars**
   see p95
1. **Specialist Shops**
   see p96
1. **Galleries and Antiques Shops**
   see p97

Impressive façade of the Hofburg palace in Central Vienna

1 The Hofburg

The former imperial palace may have relinquished its regal position after Austria became a republic in 1918, but the elegance of days gone by is still tangible *(see pp16–21)*.

2 Postsparkasse

MAP Q3 ■ Georg-Coch-Platz 2
■ Closed to the public

In the Postsparkasse building (the post office savings bank), Otto Wagner *(see p122)* implemented his principles of combining functionalism with appealing design. Stone panels fixed to the external walls with metal rivets led to the building's nickname "a box of nails" among locals.

Dürer's *Hare* (1502) at the Albertina

3 Albertina

MAP M5 ■ Albertinaplatz 1
■ U-Bahn Karlsplatz, Stephansplatz
■ Open 10am–6pm daily (until 9pm Wed & Fri) ■ Adm (free for under 19s)
■ www.albertina.at

The Hall of Muses and Rococo Room are two of the most magnificent of the 20 Habsburg State Rooms found in the Albertina palace. The palace houses seven major art collections, ranging from contemporary art to graphic, architectural and photographic art, along with period fabrics and costumes.

4 Ruprechtskirche
MAP N2 ■ Ruprechtsplatz ■
Open 10am–noon & 3–5pm Mon–Fri
This church boasts the title of Vienna's oldest place of worship, built in the 9th century after the fall of Vindobona (see p48) as part of the settlements within the Roman city walls. The stone building was the city's main church until the end of the 12th century, when Stephansdom became Vienna's most important centre of worship. Both east windows date back to the 13th century and have survived the ages untouched as Vienna's oldest works of stained glass.

Stunning exterior of Stephansdom

5 Stephansdom
At the geographical epicentre of the city, the spectacular Gothic St Stephen's Cathedral dominates the skyline with its towers and its 137-m (450-ft) spire (see pp12–15).

6 Anker Uhr
MAP N2 ■ Hoher Markt 10/11
The Anker Uhr clock spans two wings of an insurance company building and was installed between 1911 and 1917 by Franz von Matsch. Every day 12 pairs of figures, each symbolizing a period in Vienna's history, step forward on the hour. At noon, all 12 figures parade across the bridge.

JEWISH VIENNA

The Jewish Quarter centres around the "city temple" synagogue, built in 1825 in Seitenstettengasse. Today the pretty district is more famous for its bars and restaurants than for the Jewish community. Many Jews have moved to the Karmeliter quarter of the 2nd district.

7 Lo-oshaus
MAP L3 ■ Michaelerplatz 3
■ **Open 8am–3pm Mon–Wed & Fri, 8am–5:30pm Thu**
No other building triggered so much controversy in Vienna as the Looshaus, completed in 1911. Emperor Franz Joseph thought the functional building ruined the square's look and had the curtains closed at his Hofburg palace to avoid looking at it. Four floors are covered in green marble but the building's plain upper floors caused uproar. Today it is home to a bank.

8 Donnerbrunnen
MAP M4 ■ Neuer Markt
The centrepiece of the Neuer Markt is Georg Raphael Donner's fountain (1737–9) with an allegory of Providentia, the divine providence, accompanied by four cherubs towering over a pool (see p63). They are surrounded by four figures representing the rivers Traun, Enns, March and Ybbs. Regarded improper, the naked statues were removed during Maria Theresa's reign but they were replaced with replicas in the 19th century. The originals are now in the Lower Belvedere.

Neuer Markt's Donnerbrunnen

9 Burgtheater

MAP K2 ■ Universitäts-ring 2 ■ Guided tours 3pm daily; call 01 514 44 41 40 ■ Adm

The Burg, as this is affectionately called by the Viennese, was among the first theatres to be built in the German-speaking world. Gottfried Semper and Carl von Hasenauer designed this spectacular building with its Renaissance façade over a period of 14 years (1874–88). On its completion, the Court Theatre, founded in 1776, moved into the new building on the Ringstrasse. A grand staircase with frescoes by Gustav Klimt and his brother Ernst leads from the foyer to the auditorium *(see p71)*.

The Burgtheater's splendid staircase

10 Misrachi-Haus

MAP M2 ■ Judenplatz 8 ■ Open 10am–6pm Sun–Thu, 10am–5pm Fri ■ Adm (free for under 18s) ■ www.jmw.at

During the construction of a Holocaust memorial by British artist Rachel Whiteread on Judenplatz in 2000, the remains of a medieval synagogue were discovered. The excavation site is open to the public and a museum is devoted to the life, work and religion of the city's medieval Jewish community. You can also take a virtual walk around the 15th-century Jewish quarter.

A DAY'S STROLL IN CENTRAL VIENNA

▶ MORNING

Begin the day at the magnificent **Stephansdom** *(see pp12–15)*. Catch the morning sun beaming through the medieval windows, and stroll around the cathedral's Gothic features. It is well worth climbing the South Tower or taking the lift up the North Tower for stunning views over the rooftops. For a mid-morning break, head to the far end of the square and enjoy a cup of tea in **Haas & Haas** *(see p96)*.

Wander the narrow streets around the cathedral but arrive at Hoher Markt at noon to watch the historic Viennese figures of the **Anker Uhr** march by.

There are many places to have lunch, but on a sunny day pick **DO & CO Stephansplatz** *(see p99)* overlooking the cathedral.

AFTERNOON

Spend the early afternoon in Graben and Kohlmarkt, exploring antiques shops and galleries, until you reach the **Hofburg** palace *(see pp16–21)*. With its various collections, select those that interest you most, but don't miss the state apartments where Emperor Franz Joseph lived.

Leave the palace through the Michaeler Gate, then pass the **Looshaus**, before treating yourself to a piece of Sachertorte and a coffee at **Café Demel** *(see p98)*.

Finally, if you're visiting in winter, take tram 1 from Karlsplatz to Schwedenplatz to admire the floodlit buildings by night.

See map on pp90–91 ←

The Best of the Rest

1 Franziskanerplatz
MAP N4 ▪ Franziskanerplatz

This charming square is home to the Franziskanerkirche *(see p55)*, pretty houses and the Moses fountain (1798).

2 Altes Rathaus
MAP N2 ▪ Wipplingerstrasse 8
▪ Closed to the public

The Habsburgs confiscated this palace in 1316 from Otto von Haymo, who had conspired against them. It functioned as the town hall until 1883.

3 Kirche am Hof
MAP M2 ▪ Am Hof 7

Emperor Ferdinand III's widow had this monumental church built in 1662. It is more reminiscent of a palace than a place of worship.

4 Heiligenkreuzerhof
MAP P3 ▪ Schönlaterngasse

Founded in the Middle Ages as a monastery, this building now plays host to the city's arts college.

5 Peterskirche
MAP M3 ▪ Petersplatz

This Baroque church has a dramatic and ornate high altar and frescoes by Johann Michael Rottmayr.

Akademie der Wissenschaften interior

6 Akademie der Wissenschaften
MAP P3 ▪ Dr-Ignaz-Seipel-Platz
▪ Open 9am–5pm Mon–Fri ▪ Adm

This ornate Rococo building (1755) was formerly the site of Vienna University. The Academy of Sciences hall staged the premiere of Joseph Haydn's *The Creation* in 1808.

7 Pestsäule
MAP M3 ▪ Graben

After a plague epidemic that killed more than 100,000 came to an end in 1679, Emperor Leopold I had this Baroque monument installed, dedicating it to the Holy Trinity.

8 Börse
MAP L1 ▪ Schottenring 16

Once the home of the Vienna Stock Exchange, this Theophil von Hansen Classicist building, built 1874–7, is now used by the government.

9 Kapuzinerkirche
MAP M4 ▪ Neuer Markt

Built in 1618, the simple design of this church is in line with the Capuchin order's doctrine. Emperor Matthias (1557–1619) established a crypt for the Habsburgs here *(see p65)*.

10 Minoritenkirche
MAP L3 ▪ Minoritenplatz 2

When Duke Leopold VI returned safely from a crusade in 1219, he built a church on this site. Its medieval character is still visible.

Façade of the Baroque Peterskirche

→ *See map on pp90–91*

Clubs and Bars

1 American Bar
MAP N4 ■ Kärntner Strasse 10
In a simple yet sophisticated Adolf Loos building, this bar is one of the most beautiful nightspots in town. It also serves delicious cocktails.

2 Planter's Club
MAP C4 ■ Zelinkagasse 4
This colonial-style bar, with its luxurious furniture and teak wood panelling, evokes a tea plantation house. You can choose from more than 300 whiskies, 90 rums and many mouthwatering cocktails.

3 Bermuda Bräu
MAP P2 ■ Rabensteig 6
This bustling pub, in an area known as the Bermuda Triangle, is renowned for its draught beer served in clay jugs, as well as its variety of bottled beers. There's a dance floor in the basement.

4 Palmenhaus
This renovated imperial greenhouse hosts a stylish restaurant and bar with fine Austrian wines and occasional live DJ nights. The real star, however, is the glass building itself (see p99).

5 Volksgarten
MAP K4 ■ Burgring 1
The Volksgarten is one of the city's most established party zones, with a varied mix of music – soul, house, hip-hop and funk. There's also a fabulous garden in summer.

6 Onyx Bar
MAP N3 ■ Haas-Haus, Stephansplatz 12, 7th floor
Vienna's in-crowd gathers in this bar with its fine view of Stephansdom (see pp12–15). Snacks, cocktails and groovy background music are on offer.

7 Havana Club
MAP N6 ■ Mahlerstrasse 11
A great Cuban atmosphere for salsa fanatics and lashings of rum attract a crowd of locals and expats. Each day has its own dance theme and drinks menu.

8 Jazzland
MAP N2 ■ Franz-Josefs-Kai 29
Housed in a 500-year-old cellar, this popular and lively venue is the oldest jazz club in Austria. It hosts live music six nights a week.

9 Roter Engel
MAP P2 ■ Rabensteig 5
Music is the speciality of this bar, with Viennese artists playing everything from rock to pop, funk and soul every Monday to Thursday.

10 Skybar
MAP N4 ■ Kärntner Strasse 19
Popular among the well-to-do young Viennese, this place has a great vibe and a view over Vienna's rooftops. There's a good selection of cocktails.

The stylish Skybar has great city views

Specialist Shops

① Haas & Haas
MAP N3 ▪ Stephansplatz 4

Just behind Stephansdom, this shop offers more than 200 assorted fruit teas, black teas, herbal teas and many tea accessories. The marzipan sweets and chocolates are divine.

② Xocolat
MAP L2 ▪ Freyung 2, in the Palais Ferstel

Everything in this little shop revolves around chocolate, with more than 120 varieties from all over the world, as well as books on the subject.

The tempting interior of Xocolat

③ Doblinger
MAP M4 ▪ Dorotheergasse 10

This music publishing house, which has been in business for 125 years, has every music score a musician can dream of. Be it classical or contemporary music, Doblinger has it.

④ Mayr & Fessler
MAP N4 ▪ Kärntner Strasse 37

This is the best address for top-of-the-range fountain pens, as well as diaries and organizers. It has a wide range of Italian writing and wrapping paper as well as notebooks and accessories.

⑤ Gmundner Ceramics
MAP D2 ▪ Stadiongasse 7

Austrian hand-painted pottery is produced at Gmunden in Upper Austria. The traditional green-on-white decoration looks sloshed-on, but perfect. This shop offers a wide range of wares and patterns just outside the Ring behind Parliament.

⑥ Shakespeare & Co
MAP N2 ▪ Sterngasse 2

This tiny bookshop has a lot of character and is the best place to go for contemporary English literature. There are also very good travel and poetry sections.

⑦ Knize
MAP M3 ▪ Graben 13

Custom-made clothing has been the focus of this elegant establishment for nearly 150 years. The shop itself is internationally admired, as Adolf Loos turned it into a masterpiece in 1910.

⑧ Loden Plankl
MAP L3 ▪ Michaelerplatz 6

This old family business offers traditional Austrian clothing ranging from Loden coats and jackets to beautiful Dirndl dresses and Lederhosen (leather trousers). It also stocks modern variations of traditional garments.

⑨ Augarten Flagship Store
MAP M4 ▪ Spiegelgasse 3

The porcelain at the city outlet of Vienna's historic factory ranges from fine tableware to Wiener Werkstätte designs and modern objets d'art.

⑩ Meinl am Graben
MAP M3 ▪ Am Graben 19

One of Vienna's best delicatessens, this adjoins the restaurant of the same name (see p99) and has a great selection of chocolates, dessert wines and coffees.

Hamper of goodies from Meinl am Graben

Galleries and Antiques Shops

Inside the Dorotheum Auction House

① Dorotheum Auction House
MAP M4 ■ Dorotheergasse 17
■ www.dorotheum.at

Vienna is well known for its antiques, and Dorotheergasse is one of the main areas to head for if this is your interest. At the city's main auction house, in operation since 1907, you can buy everything from antique furniture to jewellery and paintings.

② Alte Kunst und Militaria
MAP M4 ■ Plankengasse 7
■ www.militaria-koeck.at

Books, guns, sabers, medals and old uniforms from past military campaigns are stocked here.

③ Wissenschaftliches Kabinett
MAP M4 ■ Spiegelgasse 23
■ www.wisskab.com

This is a fascinating place to browse unique objects such as antique surgical saws, phrenology skulls and chess pieces.

④ Galerie Ambiente
MAP N3 ■ Lugeck 1
■ www.ambientegalerieambiente.at

Beautiful and innovative furniture, from Viennese designers and manufacturers such as Josef

Hoffmann and Thonet, is sold at Ambiente. They can also arrange shipping to get your goods sent directly home.

⑤ Antiquariat Inlibris
MAP J3 ■ Rathausstrasse 19
■ www.inlibris.at

Scientific books, early prints and Austrian memorabilia are just some of the specialities at this antiquarian bookshop, established in 1883.

⑥ Wiener Interieur
MAP M4 ■ Dorotheergasse 14
■ www.wiener-interieur.at

Situated among Dorotheergasse's many galleries and antiques shops, Wiener Interieur has beautiful jewellery from the beginning of the 20th century up to the 1960s. This is a gem-lover's paradise.

⑦ Galerie Hofstätter
MAP M4 ■ Bräunerstrasse 7
■ www.galerie-hofstaetter.com

This gallery organizes several major exhibitions a year of Austrian postwar and contemporary artists.

⑧ Galerie Hilger
MAP M4 ■ Dorotheergasse 5
■ www.hilger.at

Early 20th-century art and a variety of contemporary Austrian and international artists are shown in nine exhibitions a year.

⑨ Galerie Charim
MAP M4 ■ Dorotheergasse 12
■ www.charimgalerie.at

This gallery in the former Palais Gatterburg specializes in Austrian art, including new media and object art, as well as photography.

⑩ Sonja Reisch
MAP M3 ■ Bräunerstrasse 10
■ www.antiquitaeten-reisch.com

Silver- and tableware, as well as glass and decorative objects from the Biedermeier era, are sold at this shop.

See map on pp90–91 ←

Cafés and Tearooms

1 Café Demel
MAP M3 ▪ Kohlmarkt 14

An opulent interior and central location makes Demel an ideal rest stop for snacks or pastries *(see p78)*.

2 Café Hawelka
MAP M3 ▪ Dorotheergasse 6

Open until 1am on weekends, Hawelka is dark with old-world decor inside. Don't ask for a menu – there isn't one – but do try the sweet rolls, the best in Vienna *(see p79)*.

3 Café Diglas
MAP P2 ▪ Fleischmarkt 16

A charming, small traditional café, Diglas sells mouthwatering cakes and you can even watch some being made in the historic bakery *(see p78)*.

4 Café Hofburg
MAP L4 ▪ Innerer Burghof 1

Expect sumptuous elegance and flawless service at this regal address where year-round terrace seating overlooking the Hofburg palace's inner courtyard offers a window on 600 years of Habsburg history.

5 Café Landtmann
MAP K2 ▪ Universitätsring 4

This is a temple to the Viennese concept of a traditional coffee house, with service – and prices – to match. There's a small street-side terrace for dining al fresco in good weather, and subdued elegance inside. It's an experience not to be missed *(see p78)*.

6 Café Bräunerhof
MAP M4 ▪ Stallburggasse 2

With live classical music on Saturdays and a top collection of English newspapers, this place is seldom crowded. It's traditional, but simple rather than ornate in style, and less expensive than other tourist spots *(see p79)*.

7 Café Schwartzenberg
MAP N6 ▪ Kärtner Ring 17

Instead of tourists, this distinguished café has long catered to businessmen. The oldest café on the Ringstrasse, it offers a huge choice of teas.

8 Café Prückel
MAP Q3 ▪ Stubenring 24

A highly popular reworking of the traditional coffee house in 1950s retro design, Prückel *(see p79)* is just across the street from MAK, the Museum of Applied Arts.

9 Demmers Teehaus
MAP K2 ▪ Mölker Bastei 5

The tearoom is part of a shop with more than 300 specialist teas. As well as tea, it serves snacks such as scones, cakes and sandwiches.

10 Café Central
MAP L2 ▪ Herrengasse 14

This café modestly claims to be the "true centre" of Vienna, and the lofty vaulted ceilings are said to contain the ego of Sigmund Freud *(see p78)*.

Vaulted ceilings of Café Central

Places to Eat

PRICE CATEGORIES

For a three-course meal for one with half a bottle of wine (or equivalent meal), taxes and extra charges.

€ under €35 €€ €35–70 €€€ over €70

1 Restaurant im Hotel Ambassador
MAP N4 ■ Kärntnerstrasse 22 ■ 01 961 610 ■ €€€

A menu ranging from game and traditional Viennese favourites to fish and meat dishes is served in the sumptuous surroundings of one of the best international hotels (see p76).

2 Steirereck
MAP Q4 ■ Meierei im Stadtpark ■ 01 713 31 68 ■ Closed Sat & Sun ■ €€€

One of the most highly rated Austrian restaurants makes for an essential dining experience (see p76).

Stylish interior of Fabios

3 Fabios
MAP M3 ■ Tuchlauben 6 ■ 01 532 22 22 ■ €€€

Sleek and contemporary, this Italian restaurant is popular among Vienna's glitterati and is one of the city's trendiest dining spots.

4 Palmenhaus
MAP M5 ■ Burggarten 1 ■ 01 533 10 33 ■ €€

This Art Nouveau conservatory offers great views and good food. There's also dancing on weekend evenings (see p95).

DO & CO Stephansplatz

5 DO & CO Stephansplatz
MAP N3 ■ Stephansplatz 12 ■ 01 535 39 69 ■ €€€

This very stylish restaurant offers a selection of the best dishes, ranging from Viennese cuisine to sushi and Thai food (see p77).

6 Silvio Nickol
MAP P4 ■ Coburgbastei 4 ■ 01 518 18 800 ■ €€€

Famous for its tasting menus, Silvio Nickol has an international reputation for its exquisite contemporary fare.

7 Plachutta
MAP N3 ■ Wollzeile 38 ■ 01 512 15 77 ■ €€

This traditional Viennese place is known for its beef dishes. Don't miss the *tafelspitz* with roasted potatoes.

8 Wrenkh
MAP N3 ■ Bauernmarkt 10 ■ 01 533 15 26 ■ Closed Sun & hols ■ €€

One of the most popular vegetarian eateries in the city (see p77).

9 Meinl am Graben
MAP M3 ■ Graben 19 ■ 01 532 33 34 ■ Closed Sun ■ €€€

Expect outstanding food and service at this flagship eatery of the Julius Meinl grocery chain (see p77).

10 Stadtbeisl Inigo
MAP P3 ■ Bäckerstrasse 18 ■ 01 512 74 51 ■ €

Viennese and international cuisine. Wine list changes every other month.

See map on pp90–91

🔟 Schottenring and Alsergrund

A large part of this area is inhabited by medical institutions, including the AKH general hospital and the Vienna medical school. This is perhaps not surprising in the area where the psychoanalyst Sigmund Freud lived and worked in the early 20th century. The Votivkirche dominates the skyline and looks across a park towards the city centre.

The famous Art Nouveau Strudlhofstiege staircase in the snow

SCHOTTENRING AND ALSERGRUND

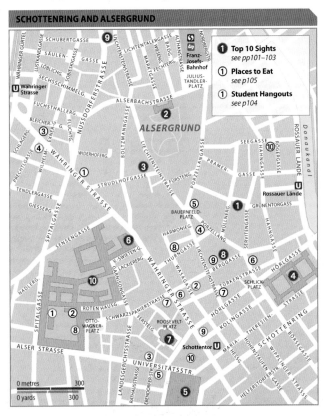

1 Top 10 Sights
see pp101–103

1 Places to Eat
see p105

1 Student Hangouts
see p104

ALSERGRUND

Ornate paintings and stucco decorations in the Servitenkirche dome

1 Servitenkirche
MAP B3 ■ Servitengasse 9
■ Open 9am–10pm daily

Although this church is slightly off the beaten track, it is well worth a visit. Built by the Servite convent along with an adjoining monastery in 1651, the interior is decorated with stucco ornaments and frescoes, but the most interesting detail is the 13th-century crucifix to the right of the high altar. Originally the "cross of gallows", it stood at the public execution place on Schlickplatz.

2 Gartenpalais Liechtenstein
MAP A3 ■ Fürstengasse 1
■ Open only for pre-booked tours on Fri (twice a month); call 01 319 57 670 ■ Adm ■ www.palaisliechtenstein.com

Built as the summer residence for the Liechtenstein family at the end of the 17th century, the Liechtenstein Garden Palace is Vienna's premier home of Baroque art. The collection includes works by many important artists, such as Raphael, Rubens and Rembrandt. The lovely formal gardens are free and open to the public (see p50).

3 Strudlhofstiege
MAP B3 ■ Strudlhofgasse/ Liechtensteinstrasse

This striking Art Nouveau outdoor double staircase, which winds its way down from Strudlhofgasse to Liechtensteinstrasse, was designed by Theodor Jäger in 1910. Two fountains, several lampposts and various ramps create a graceful impression. It became famous in 1951, when Austrian writer Heimito von Doderer published a novel named after the stairway.

4 Rossauer Kaserne
MAP B4 ■ Schlickplatz 6
■ Closed to the public

These huge barracks were created to protect Vienna from attacks from outside the city as well as revolt from within, after the revolutions that took place across Europe in 1848. Together with two other military camps, the Rossauer base formed a strategic triangle. Work on the barracks began in 1864 and was completed six years later. They became the city's police headquarters after World War II.

Memorial outside Rossauer Kaserne

Vienna University main entrance

5 Vienna University
MAP K1 ▪ Universitätsring 1
▪ Open Mon–Sat

The university was founded by Duke Rudolph IV in 1365 and today has around 60,000 students. The present building was constructed in Italian Renaissance style on a former army parade ground following plans by Heinrich Ferstel, and opened in 1884. From the entrance hall with marble columns, grand staircases lead to the lecture theatres and the library. The arcaded courtyard is lined with busts of distinguished professors and the university's eight Nobel Prize winners. The ceremony hall is decorated with frescoes by Gustav Klimt (1895).

SIGMUND FREUD

In his study of the unconscious mind, Sigmund Freud (1856–1939) divided the human psyche into three different levels (id, ego and superego) that, if unbalanced, could cause mental disorder. He observed that these problems tended to disappear after forgotten material was made conscious. His ideas were the foundation of modern psychoanalysis.

6 Josephinum
MAP B3 ▪ Währinger Strasse 25
▪ Open 10am–6pm Fri & Sat ▪ Adm

Founded by Emperor Joseph II in 1785 as a medical academy, the Josephinum first trained military doctors, and later general practitioners. Today these buildings are home to the Institute for the History of Medicine and an anatomical museum (see p57).

7 Votivkirche
MAP C3 ▪ Rooseveltplatz
▪ Open 9am–1pm & 4–6:30pm Tue–Sat, 9am–1pm Sun

This sandstone church with its charming ornate façade is part of the grand Ringstrasse. Inside there is a small museum, with gold and jewelled chalices and other sacred objects. There is also a shop on site. On Sundays, the church services are in English (see pp54–5).

The elaborate exterior of the pretty sandstone Votivkirche

8 Sigmund Freud Museum

MAP B3 ■ Berggasse 19 ■ Open 9am–5pm daily ■ Adm ■ www.freud-museum.at

The founder of psychoanalysis lived in Vienna from 1891 until 1938, when he fled from the National Socialists to London. In his spacious apartment in Berggasse, now a museum, he wrote many famous works and case histories such as *The Interpretation of Dreams*.

Exhibition at Sigmund Freud Museum

9 Schubert's House of Birth

MAP A2 ■ Nussdorfer Strasse 54 ■ Open 10am–1pm & 2–6pm Tue–Sun & public hols ■ Adm (free for under 19s and every first Sun)

Franz Schubert was born in the kitchen of this little first-floor apartment, now a museum, on 31 January 1797 and spent the first four years of his life in the property, known locally as "House of the Red Crab". The museum has information on the composer's life *(see p60)* as well as portraits by Schubert's contemporaries.

10 Altes Allgemeines Krankenhaus

MAP B2 ■ Spitalgasse 2 ■ Wards and courtyards: closed to the public

This huge hospital complex with 11 courtyards is an oasis of calm. In the late 18th century, Emperor Joseph II converted an existing house for the poor into a general hospital, which included a "birth house", a "foundling house" and a "mad house" – today a pathological museum *(see p57)*. The complex is now part of the Vienna University campus.

A DAY IN VIENNA'S STUDENT DISTRICT

▶ MORNING

Start your day at **Vienna University**, exploring the marble entrance hall and the courtyard. Then head towards the beautiful **Votivkirche**, passing through **Sigmund Freud Park** *(see p63)*. Walk up Alser Strasse until you reach the **Altes Allgemeines Krankenhaus**, the former general hospital. For a break, choose one of the many pubs in the large first courtyard, amid crowds of students.

Head to courtyard 13, where the **Pathologisch-Anatomisches Museum** *(see p57)* is situated. Cut your way to Strudlhofgasse and stride down **Strudlhofstiege** *(see p101)*, where you can already spot the **Gartenpalais Liechtenstein** *(see p101)*. In Porzellangasse you will find several places for lunch.

AFTERNOON

On your way to the **Sigmund Freud Museum**, ensure you pass by **Servitenkirche** *(see p101)* and stop for a glimpse of the Baroque interior. Give yourself enough time to have a look around Dr Freud's apartment and consulting rooms. For a break and a cup of coffee, **Café Berg** *(see p104)* just across the road is a great place to rest your feet and gather your thoughts. Then visit the collection of 18th-century anatomical wax models in the **Josephinum**.

You can round the day off with a visit to Votiv Kino, an arts cinema that shows independent films in the original language *(Währinger Strasse 12; 317 35 71)*.

See map on p100 ←

Student Hangouts

① Stiegl-Ambulanz
MAP C2 ■ University Campus, Alser Strasse 4

Open all year round, Stiegl-Ambulanz offers traditional Viennese food at reasonable prices. It also has a wide range of beers.

② Café Berg
MAP C3 ■ Berggasse 8

A trendy hangout with cosy seating, next door to the LGBT bookshop Löwenherz, serving healthy and simple dishes.

③ Cafeteria Maximilian
MAP K1 ■ Universitätsstrasse 2

Just a stone's throw from Vienna University, this cafeteria serves simple comfort food, attracting hordes of young people, many of whom stay a while to socialize.

④ Statt-Beisl WUK
MAP B2 ■ Währinger Strasse 59

This former 19th-century locomotive factory has been cleverly converted into a cultural centre and operates a café and restaurant.

⑤ Zwillings-Gwölb
MAP K1 ■ Universitätsstrasse 5

Located just behind the university is Zwillings-Gwölb – meaning "twin vaults." On the ground floor, there is a pleasant café-type restaurant, whilst the cellar is home to an atmospheric pub.

⑥ Café Votiv
MAP C3 ■ Währinger Strasse 12

The trendy café within the Votiv cinema is popular with students as well as, of course, cinemagoers before and after film screenings.

⑦ Charlie P's
MAP C3 ■ Währinger Strasse 3

One of several Irish pubs dotted around the city, Charlie P's has a particularly lively atmosphere. Fish and chips and Guinness are essential parts of the traditional menu.

⑧ Gangl
MAP C2 ■ University Campus, Alser Strasse 4

Beer on tap, toasted sandwiches and a cosy atmosphere (as well as seating outside in summer) attract a loyal crowd of students here.

⑨ Café Stein
MAP C3 ■ Währinger Strasse 6–8

This spot has seating inside and out, and offers a good view of the nearby Votivkirche (see p102). This is a great choice for a traditional breakfast, and also hosts various cultural events.

⑩ Sigmund Freud Park
MAP K1

On a sunny day the verdant lawns of Sigmund Freud Park, just opposite the university buildings, are inhabited by crowds of students studying, picnicking, sunbathing and debating the issues of the day (see p63).

Relaxing in Sigmund Freud Park

Places to Eat

1 Kim
MAP C3 ■ Währinger Strasse 46
■ 664 425 88 66 ■ Closed Sun, Mon
■ €€€

Sohyi Kim has moved to this tiny, trendy venue, bringing her Korean fusion to just ten diners at a time. Most dishes are vegetarian (see p77).

2 Universitätsbräuhaus
MAP J1 ■ University Campus, Alser Strasse 4 ■ 01 409 1815 ■ No credit cards ■ €

Simple but tasty dishes served in the pharmacy of the old hospital.

6 Oasia
MAP B4 ■ Schlickgasse 2
■ 01 310 01 70 ■ Closed Sun ■ €

Dim sum is a speciality at this modern Asian-fusion restaurant with a sushi bar and open kitchen.

7 Der Wiener Deewan
MAP C3 ■ Liechtensteinstrasse 10 ■ 01 925 11 85 ■ Closed Sun ■ €€

The Pakistani menu has garnered rave reviews. Eat as much as you want and pay as little as you like.

8 Dreiklang
MAP C3 ■ Wasagasse 28 ■ 01 310 17 03 ■ Closed Sat & Sun ■ No credit cards ■ €

This vegetarian restaurant uses only organic products for its dishes and serves a midday menu.

Chandeliered interior of Café Weimar

3 Café Weimar
MAP B2 ■ Währinger Strasse 68
■ 01 317 12 06 ■ €

This traditional café-restaurant with a pianist serves hot and cold snacks and offers a set lunch at midday.

4 D'Landsknecht
MAP B3 ■ Porzellangasse 13
■ 01 317 43 48 ■ Closed Sat & Sun ■ €

A long-established local favourite: expect hearty portions of authentic Austrian soups and main dishes at moderate prices here.

5 Gasthaus Wickerl
MAP B3 ■ Porzellangasse 24a
■ 01 317 74 89 ■ Closed Sun D ■ No credit cards ■ €€

A very authentic Viennese restaurant with good Austrian cuisine.

9 Ragusa
MAP B3 ■ Berggasse 15 ■ 01 317 15 77 ■ Closed Sun ■ €€

Dalmatian cooking (specialities include fish and seafood) in a cosy atmosphere with outdoor seating.

10 Stomach
MAP B3 ■ Seegasse 26 ■ 01 310 20 99 ■ Closed Mon & Tue ■ €€

Enjoy modern food in one of the nicest outdoor dining areas.

Stomach's pretty outdoor courtyard

See map on p100

TOP10 MuseumsQuartier, Town Hall and Neubau

The areas around the MuseumsQuartier, Town Hall and Neubau represent both the political centre of Austria and the cultural heart of the capital, being home to a mix of government bureaus, world-class exhibition spaces and funky, Bohemian boutiques in character-packed cobbled streets. This is where conventional Vienna and the city's edgier, arty side meet among restaurants, shops, vintage stores, museums and galleries.

Statues outside the Parliament building

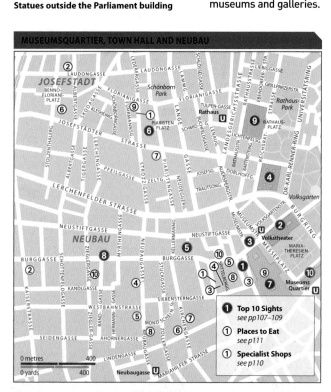

MUSEUMSQUARTIER, TOWN HALL AND NEUBAU

1	**Top 10 Sights** *see pp107–109*
1	**Places to Eat** *see p111*
1	**Specialist Shops** *see p110*

1 Spittelberg
MAP J5

The charming Spittelberg area consists of a few cobbled, narrow streets with pretty houses and spouting fountains between Breite Gasse, Siebensterngasse, Sigmundsgasse and Burggasse. In the 18th century the area was full of hovels, gambling dens and brothels, but by the 19th century these had been closed down and, over time, the district became increasingly derelict. The city authorities only began to recognize the area's charm in the 1970s, and today it's a thriving enclave of galleries, handicraft shops and cosy pubs.

2 Naturhistorisches Museum
MAP K4 ■ Burgring 7 ■ Open 9am–6:30pm Wed–Mon (to 9pm Wed) ■ Adm (free for under 19s) ■ www.nhm-wien.ac.at

Often voted among the world's top ten museums and built as a mirror image of its more famous neighbour, the Kunsthistorisches Museum, the Natural History Museum opened in 1889. The fascinating collections of archaeology, natural history and geology grew out of Emperor Franz Stephan's 1748 collection of natural curiosities. The museum's splendid interior was designed to enhance the exhibits, which today amount to more than 20 million pieces. The most precious rarities are the 25,000-year-old Venus of Willendorf figurine and a "bouquet of jewels" given to Francis I by his wife Maria Theresa.

Naturhistorisches Museum exhibits

Lavish interior of the Volkstheater

3 Volkstheater
MAP J4 ■ Arthur-Schnitzler-Platz 1 ■ www.volkstheater.at

The Volkstheater ("people's theatre") was established in 1889 as a counterpart to the imperial Burgtheater (see p93). Its aim was to offer classic and modern drama to a larger audience at reasonable prices. Constructed by the acclaimed theatre architects Ferdinand Fellner and Hermann Helmer, the theatre was designed in Historicist style and fitted with the latest technology, such as electric lighting. With just under 1,000 seats, it is among the largest German-language theatres in the world.

4 Parliament
MAP K3 ■ Dr-Karl-Renner-Ring 3 ■ Interior closed to the public due to extensive renovation

This building (1873–83) was designed by the architect Theophil von Hansen in Greek style to celebrate the cradle of democracy. Two ramps lined by statues of Greek philosophers lead to the main entrance. The first Austrian Republic was declared here in 1918.

5 Sankt-Ulrichs-Platz
MAP E2

At the heart of this charming cobbled square is St Ulrich's church, which is surrounded by a pretty ensemble of patrician houses dating back to various periods. At No. 5 is a rare example of a Renaissance house, while the Baroque edifice at No. 27 bears a statue of St Nepomuk, who gave the house its name. During the Turkish Siege of 1683, Kara Mustafa's troops pitched their tents on this square.

Sculpture outside St Ulrich's church

6 Piaristenkirche Maria Treu
MAP D2 ▪ Jodok Fink Platz
▪ Open during church services
▪ www.mariatreu.at

Walking into narrow Piaristengasse from Josefstädter Strasse, the charming square on the left comes as a surprise. The Piaristenkirche Maria Treu (Maria Treu Church) here was built from 1719 onwards to a design by Lukas von Hildebrandt. The dome's frescoes are by the Austrian Baroque artist Franz Anton Maulbertsch (1752). The column in front of the church was installed in 1713 to give thanks for the end of a plague epidemic.

7 MuseumsQuartier
The former imperial stables have been imaginatively transformed into a vast complex of museums and entertainment venues that shouldn't be missed (see pp34–5).

8 Neubau
MAP C2

The Neubau district attracts a steady stream of hipster tourists to studios selling bold artworks, cool cafés, vintage clothes boutiques and independent stores full of wacky wares and eco-fashion. In the last decade, Neubau's arty, progressive character has emerged as "Vienna's Berlin" and to stroll around the galleries and kooky outlets in its backstreets is to experience the city's trendy side.

An eclectic mishmash of shops sells everything from modern textiles, bespoke jewellery and second-hand fetish gear to gourmet foods, bizarre kitchen gadgets, photographic art and multicoloured retro frocks. Fanning north from the Mariahilfer Strasse towards the Lerchenfelder Strasse, Neubau's stores run along Neubaugasse and Lindengasse, with the MuseumsQuartier marking the district's eastern border.

9 Neues Rathaus
MAP J2 ▪ Rathausplatz ▪ Tours with audio guides in English 1pm Mon, Wed & Fri ▪ www.wien.gv.at

The Neo-Gothic town hall, with its spires, loggias and stone rosettes in the pointed windows, was built by Friedrich von Schmidt in 1883 to express the inhabitants' pride in their city at that time. The impressive building has seven arcaded courtyards and 1,575 rooms, where the Vienna

City Council and the mayor have their offices. All year round, various festivals take place on the square in front of the Rathaus, ranging from a Christmas market to a music film festival in summer *(see pp86–7)*. Don't miss the opportunity to see the building at night, when floodlights spectacularly highlight the façade.

Kunsthistorisches Museum painting

10 Kunsthistorisches Museum

Vienna's Kunsthistorisches Museum is home to an impressive collection of artistic treasures, spanning the centuries from the ancient world to the modern day *(see pp22–5)*.

RINGSTRASSE

The Ringstrasse encircles the city's first district and is one of the world's most elegant avenues. In 1857 Franz Joseph I ordered Vienna's medieval strongholds be torn down and the city be given an imperial face with grand edifices. Palaces were then built along the new boulevard that was officially opened in 1865.

The MuseumsQuartier at night

A WALK AROUND THE MUSEUMSQUARTIER

▶ MORNING

Begin your day at the **Neues Rathaus**, then stroll along the Ringstrasse towards **Parliament** *(see p107)*. Once you have taken in these political gems, you are then free to explore the city's wonderful museums.

The museum highlights are the **Kunsthistorisches Museum** and **Naturhistorisches Museum** *(see p107)*, and you could easily spend a full day in each of these places, so select your main areas of interest and concentrate on those collections. Have a morning coffee in the museums themselves – the cafés in both are excellent and offer a great view of the museums' lower floors.

Walk across the square to the **MuseumsQuartier** and wander around the many courtyards. Before embarking on another museum, stop for lunch in any of the four restaurants in the complex – all of them offer equally delicious food.

AFTERNOON

After lunch, visit **mumok** *(see p34)* and the **Leopold Museum** *(see p35)*, before leaving the complex through gates 6 or 7. These lead you straight to the **Volkstheater** *(see p107)*. Make your way up Burggasse and the **Spittelberg** area *(see p107)* spills out to your left, where you can look around the shops and galleries.

After dark, return to the Neues Rathaus to see it lit up against the night sky.

See map on p106 ←

Specialist Shops

1 Quendler's feine Weine
MAP D2 ■ Lederergasse 17

This is the top address in Vienna for fine red and white Austrian wines, including Riesling, as well as wines from around the world.

2 Grand Cru
MAP E2 ■ Kaiserstrasse 67

This shop offers a great selection of coffees, both Viennese and international, as well as delicious chocolates with a variety of tasty fillings.

Tasty wares on display at Grand Cru

3 Teehaus Artee
MAP E2 ■ Siebensterngasse 4

Offering a wide range of teas, complemented by stylish teapots and cups from all over the world, Artee is an elegant place to shop and sample tea. Authentic Asian food, with dim sum variations, is served all day.

4 Bag and Art
MAP E2 ■ Neubaugasse 49

Specialists in leather handbags and leather gloves, Bag and Art also hosts changing exhibitions in the shop.

Stylish furniture at Das Möbel

5 Mastnak
MAP E2 ■ Neubaugasse 31

One of two shops, jumbling everything from drawing pencils to schoolbags to wrapping paper into a small emporium. It also does printing and copying.

6 Geschirr Niessner
MAP E2 ■ Kirchengasse 9A

This family-run kitchen equipment emporium has plenty of vintage products, including English and Austrian porcelain.

7 Vinoe
MAP D2 ■ Piaristengasse 35

The specialist in wines from Lower Austria stocks 400 varieties, which can be delivered.

8 Shu!
MAP E2 ■ Neubaugasse 34

Designer shoes in unusual colours, with extraordinary heels or bizarre buckles: Shu! is a footwear paradise.

9 Komische Künst
MAP K5 ■ Museumsplatz 1

In the heart of the MuseumsQuartier, this place is great if you're looking for a laugh. There are cartoons and comic books with illustrations as well as more "serious" academic works on the anatomy of the funny bone.

10 Das Möbel
MAP E2 ■ Burggasse 10

A mixture between a furniture gallery, café and restaurant where you can test out the furniture while having a drink or a meal. The design of the interior changes every three months.

Places to Eat

PRICE CATEGORIES

For a three-course meal for one with half a bottle of wine (or equivalent meal), taxes and extra charges.

€ under €35 ■ €€ €35–70 ■ €€€ over €70

1 Amerling Beisl
MAP E2 ■ Stiftgasse 8 ■ 01 526 16 60 ■ €

This Biedermeier-style courtyard garden, open in summer, serves Viennese comfort food, including noodles and dumplings.

2 Die Wäscherei
MAP C1 ■ Albertgasse 49 ■ 01 409 23 75 11 ■ €

This former laundry is one of the hot spots in the area. It has a delicious brunch menu at weekends, but book ahead – it's very popular (see p76).

3 Plutzer Bräu
MAP E2 ■ Schrankgasse 2 ■ 01 526 12 15 ■ €

A pub serving burgers, with huge TV screens for sports fans. In summer there is seating outside.

4 Tian Bistro
MAP E2 ■ Schrankgasse 4 ■ 01 526 94 91 ■ Closed Mon ■ €€

The shaded gardens here provide respite on hot days and it's an oasis for vegetarians in meat-eating Vienna.

5 Zu ebener Erde und erster Stock
MAP E2 ■ Burggasse 13 ■ 01 523 62 54 ■ Closed Sat & Sun ■ €€

On the ground and first floors of a beautiful Biedermeier-style house, this eatery serves creative and traditional Austrian cuisine and fine wines.

6 Prinz Ferdinand
MAP D1 ■ Bennoplatz 2 ■ 01 402 94 17 ■ Closed Mon ■ €€

A typical Viennese restaurant with classic Austrian specialities. In summer there is romantic seating underneath trees on the square.

7 Figar
MAP E2 ■ Kirchengasse 18 ■ 01 890 99 47 ■ Closed Thu ■ €

Great brunches and many vegetarian choices. Figar is something of a hipster hangout – it is open until 2am and smoking is allowed inside – but there is an outdoor patio in summer.

Charming interior of Witwe Bolte

8 Witwe Bolte
MAP J5 ■ Gutenberggasse 13 ■ 01 523 14 50 ■ €€

This cosy spot in the Spittelberg area has outdoor seating in summer, a delightful interior and offers refined Viennese cuisine and Austrian wines.

9 Tunnel
MAP D1 ■ Florianigasse 39 ■ 01 405 34 65 ■ No credit cards ■ €

A mix of international food and plenty of Asian dishes feature on the menu here. In the evenings, there is live music until it closes at 2am.

10 Gaumenspiel
MAP E1 ■ Zieglergasse 54 ■ 01 526 11 08 ■ Closed Sun ■ €€

Inventive dishes such as lobster ravioli are served on a regularly changing menu at Gaumenspiel.

See map on p106 ←

🔟 Opera and Naschmarkt

This is a multifaceted area, which features a variety of architectural landmarks standing regally alongside the colourful activity of the Naschmarkt. It is characterized by great buildings of various styles such as the historic State Opera House and the Academy of Fine Arts, as well as the finest examples of Viennese Art Nouveau with the Secession Building and two stunning Otto Wagner houses on Linke Wienzeile. The area is also a shoppers' paradise – Mariahilfer Strasse boasts hundreds of stores and many cafés and restaurants, while the Naschmarkt offers a different kind of retail experience. The lively market with eclectic stalls bears some resemblance to Oriental bazaars and is a delight for all the senses.

Detail from interior of the Theater an der Wien

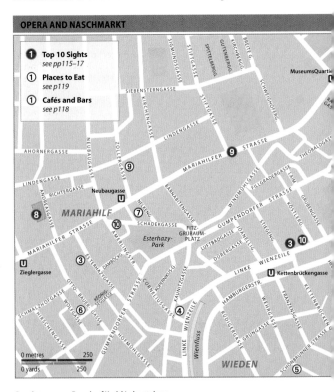

OPERA AND NASCHMARKT

1️⃣ **Top 10 Sights**
  see pp115–17

1️⃣ **Places to Eat**
  see p119

1️⃣ **Cafés and Bars**
  see p118

Previous pages Façade of Karlskirche at dawn

Grand staircase at the Staatsoper

1 Staatsoper

The Vienna State Opera House is an iconic landmark in a city that is passionate about its music. Its 300 performances a year attract an international audience, as does the annual Opera Ball, during which audience members are allowed backstage to mingle with the stars (see pp36–7).

2 Akademie der bildenden Künste Picture Collection

MAP L6 ■ Schillerplatz 3 (temporarily at Lobkowitzplatz 2) ■ Open 10am–6pm Wed–Thu ■ Adm (free for under 19s) ■ www.akbild.ac.at

When the city's medieval bastions were knocked down at the end of the 19th century and the Ringstrasse was laid out, Theophil von Hansen built an Italian Renaissance-style building on Schillerplatz in 1872–6 to house Vienna's art school. The school, founded by Peter Strudel in 1692, moved here from the Strudelhof building on the academy's completion. Due to ongoing restoration work, the painting collection has been shifted to Palais Lobkowitz (see p58).

3 Majolika Haus

MAP F3 ■ Linke Wienzeile 40

One of the finest examples of an Art Nouveau-style house was designed by the celebrated architect Otto Wagner in 1898. The house is decorated with colourful floral patterns on glazed tiles – pink roses, green leaves and blue blossoms spread across the building's surface. The windowsills bear matching floral patterns. The house is now divided into apartments with shops on the ground floor.

4 Secession Building

This late-19th-century building is a remarkable celebration of the Secessionist artistic movement founded by Gustav Klimt (see pp38–9).

Vienna Secession Building

⑤ Naschmarkt
MAP F4 ■ Between Karlsplatz and Kettenbrückengasse ■ Open 6am–7:30pm Mon–Fri, 6am–6pm Sat ■ www.naschmarkt-vienna.com

The city's largest market, bustling Naschmarkt is a colourful place with some 120 stalls. At 6am, vendors selling fruit, vegetables, flowers, meat and fish open their stalls. On Saturdays, farmers from outside the city offer their produce, and at the Saturday flea market stalls sell everything from antiques to second-hand clothing.

⑥ Theater an der Wien
MAP F3 ■ Linke Wienzeile 6 ■ 01 588 30 661 ■ Backstage tours can be pre-booked ■ www.theater-wien.at

Emanuel Schikaneder, a friend of Mozart, founded this theatre in 1801. It remained closed for many years, until it opened its doors once again in 2006 on Mozart's 250th birth anniversary. Now billed as "The New Opera House of Vienna", it stages an opera premiere every month. There is a youthful repertory company and a programme of song and youth opera called the Kammeroper or Chamber Opera. Performances of Mozart are frequent, but contemporary opera is also featured here.

The Schiller monument

A MUSICAL CITY
Vienna is inextricably connected to classical music and often referred to as the world's musical capital. The art-loving Habsburgs acted as paymasters and provided the perfect setting for a thriving musical landscape, particularly from the late 18th to the 19th centuries. Today the traditions of its past remain, but there is also a vivid scene of contemporary music in the city.

⑦ Schiller Monument
MAP L6 ■ Schillerplatz

The main focal point of Schillerplatz, the square in front of the Academy of Fine Arts, is the statue of the poet and dramatist Friedrich Schiller, sculpted by Johannes Schilling in 1876. Opposite is the Goethe monument, created by Edmund von Hellmer in 1900 *(see p52)* as a tribute to another great German-language writer.

The opulent gilded interior of the Theater an der Wien

8 Hofmobiliendepot
MAP F1 ■ Andreasgasse 7
■ Open Jan–Mar: 10am–6pm Tue–
Sun; Apr–Dec: 10am–6pm daily ■
Adm ■ www.hofmobiliendepot.at

In the Imperial Furniture Collection, established by Empress Maria Theresa in the late 18th century, all the Habsburgs' furniture was stored, repaired and kept in a good state to be distributed to imperial households when required. Today the museum tells how imperial families used to live and has thousands of exhibits – from the everyday to the highly unusual – spanning more than five centuries.

Shoppers in the Mariahilfer Strasse

9 Mariahilfer Strasse
MAP K6

After Kärntner Strasse and the Graben, this pedestrianized street is Vienna's trendiest and busiest shopping mile. Hundreds of shops and a few department stores offer fashion, books, music and electronic goods, while cafés, restaurants, ice-cream parlours and cinemas abound.

10 Wagner Haus
MAP F3 ■ Linke Wienzeile 38

Next to the Majolika Haus is another of Otto Wagner's Art Nouveau-style buildings. The six-storey house has a white plastered façade with golden stucco elements. Between the top row of windows are golden medallions with female heads, designed by Koloman Moser (1868–1918). Peacock feathers trail under the medallions reaching down to the windows below. Above the rounded corner with an iron-and-glass porch are statues of female "callers" by Othmar Schimkowitz (1864–1947).

A DAY IN THE OPERA AND NASCHMARKT AREA

▶ **MORNING**

Starting off by admiring the majestic, Neo-Renaissance **Staatsoper** *(see pp36–7)*, cut your way through Operngasse to the **Secession Building** *(see pp38–9)*. You could stare at the iconic exterior of Olbrich's Secessionist masterpiece, with its ornate dome made up of gilt laurel leaves, for hours, but the stunning *Beethoven Frieze* inside this Art Nouveau building shouldn't be missed.

For a coffee break, head for the refurbished **Café Museum** *(see p118)*, first designed by Adolf Loos in 1899.

Walk towards **Naschmarkt**, and roam the market with its variety of stalls and lively atmosphere, casting a glance over the road to the **Theater an der Wien**, the **Majolika Haus** *(see p115)* and the **Wagner Haus**.

For lunch, choose from one of the many cafés or restaurants on Naschmarkt, such as the bustling **Do An** *(see p119)*.

AFTERNOON

Make your way up to **Mariahilfer Strasse** and spend the rest of the afternoon leisurely looking around the many shops.

Stay in the area for the evening and attend a classical opera performance, either in the Staatsoper or in the Theater an der Wien. But, whichever of the two entertainment venues you choose, make sure you have booked your tickets in advance.

See map on pp114–15 ←

Cafés and Bars

1 Café Drechsler
MAP F2 ■ Linke Wienzeile 22

Elegantly remodelled by British architects Conran & Partners, this legendary coffee house has regained its mantle as the place in Vienna for a late late-night drink or an early morning breakfast.

2 Café Sperl
MAP K6
■ Gumpendorfer Strasse 11

This stylish café has been in business since the 19th century and has always had a reputation for being frequented by the city's artists, musicians, actors and nobles. It is just as popular today as it has always been (see p79).

Tasty pastry at the Café Museum

3 Barfly's Club
MAP F2 ■ Esterhazygasse 33

Situated in the Hotel Fürst Metternich, this fashionable bar serves a huge selection of cocktails, whiskies and rums, as well as offering regular live jazz and swing music.

4 Wein & Co Bar
MAP L6 ■ Linke Wienzeile 4

Just opposite the Secession Building, this trendy place is not only a wine shop but also a bar with more than 60 wines from all across the globe. It also serves Italian cuisine.

Chic interior of Wein & Co Bar

5 Naschmarkt Deli
MAP F4 ■ Naschmarkt stall 421–36

This little café set amid the bustling Naschmarkt market stalls serves excellent breakfasts all day long and offers all kinds of ethnic cuisines, from Viennese to Turkish.

6 Café Museum
MAP M5 ■ Operngasse 7

Adolf Loos's minimalist-designed coffee house makes a great place to people-watch and soak up the atmosphere while enjoying a selection of coffee and delicious cakes (see p78).

7 Tanzcafé Jenseits
MAP F2 ■ Nelkengasse 3

It would be easy to walk right past this very cosy bar but it's worth a stop. Its plush reddish decor has a slightly faded, Hollywood-of-yesteryear feel, and there is a small dance floor.

8 Der Hannes
MAP F3 ■ Pressgasse 29

This cosy coffee house located close to the colourful Naschmarkt offers late breakfasts, pancakes with a variety of toppings and fillings, and excellent beers.

9 Café Europa
MAP E2 ■ Zollergasse 8

This is as close as you'll come to an all-night American diner in Vienna, both in its ambience and its extensive menu. Sip alcoholic drinks and tuck into hearty food, served until the sun comes up (see p78).

10 Café Ritter
MAP F2 ■ Mariahilfer Strasse 73

A traditional café just off the main shopping drag, Ritter offers the obligatory variety of coffees, cakes, snacks and newspapers. It makes a great break from nearby shopping.

Places to Eat

1 Umarfisch
MAP F3 ▪ Naschmarkt Stand
76–9 ▪ 01 587 04 56 ▪ Closed Sun
▪ €€

Try the delicious oysters with a
glass of sparkling wine at this
fish restaurant.

2 Theatercafé
MAP F3 ▪ Linke Wienzeile 6 ▪ 01
585 62 62 ▪ Closed Sat & Sun ▪ €€

Serving Austrian food with Asian and
Italian influences, this place is busy
after shows at the theatre next door.

Colourful exterior of Do An at night

3 Do An
MAP F4 ▪ Naschmarkt stall 412
▪ 01 585 82 53 ▪ Closed Sun ▪ No
credit cards ▪ €

Do An prepares a varied cuisine – the
smoked tofu with sautéed courgettes,
carrots and spring onions is delicious.

4 Salzberg
MAP G2 ▪ Magdalenenstrasse
17 ▪ 01 581 62 26 ▪ €€

In a traditional setting, Salzberg
serves creative Viennese dishes and
beer specially brewed in eastern
Austria for the restaurant.

5 Zu den drei Buchteln
MAP G3 ▪ Wehrgasse 9 ▪ 01
587 83 65 ▪ Closed Sun ▪ No credit
cards ▪ €€

This friendly place serves traditional
Bohemian specialities such as yeast
cakes, known as *buchteln (see p77)*.

PRICE CATEGORIES

For a three-course meal for one with half
a bottle of wine (or equivalent meal),
taxes and extra charges.

€ under €35 €€ €35–70 €€€ over €70

6 Steman
MAP F1 ▪ Otto-Bauer Gasse 7 ▪
01 597 85 09 ▪ Closed Sat & Sun ▪ €€

Diners eat at long tables at this cosy
part-wooden-panelled restaurant
serving traditional Viennese fare
(see p77).

7 Indian Pavilion
MAP F3 ▪ Naschmarkt
74–5 ▪ 01 587 85 61
▪ Closed D and Sun ▪ €

This may well be the
smallest Indian res-
taurant in Vienna, but
it is also the best. Try
the lentil soup, then
the divine mango pickle
with a curry. Get there
early as it fills up quickly.

8 Café Amarcord
MAP F3 ▪ Rechte Wienzeile 15
▪ 01 587 47 09 ▪ No credit cards ▪ €€

This is a very relaxed place (open
until 1am) with leather sofas –
perfect after the hectic Naschmarkt.
The food is tasty and there is a wide
range of choices.

9 Restaurant Sopile
MAP F4 ▪ Paulanergasse 10
▪ 01 585 24 33 ▪ Closed Sun and
public hols ▪ €€

A Croatian restaurant with a strong
emphasis on fish dishes as well as
truffles and game. Excellent wine list.

10 Chang Asian Noodles
MAP F4 ▪ Waaggasse 1 ▪ 01 961
92 12 ▪ Closed Sun ▪ €

This modern noodle bar is always
busy. It serves simple Asian food
at reasonable prices. The weekly
lunchtime set menus are a bargain.

See map on pp114–15

🔟 From Karlskirche to the Belvedere

The area from Karlskirche to the Belvedere Palace is filled with grand mansions and summer residences from the 18th and 19th centuries. Vienna's aristocracy built their summer palaces here

because it was in the countryside but not too far from the city. Prince Eugene's summer retreat, the Belvedere, dominates the area, but there are several other ornate homes, such as the Palais Schwarzenberg and the Palais Hoyos, which are well worth a visit. Today many such buildings are embassies and some of the once private gardens are public parks. During Roman times the civil settlement of the Vindobona military camp (see p48) was situated here. The area's main roads, Landstrasser Hauptstrasse and Rennweg, follow old Roman routes.

Painted dome inside the Salesianerinnenkirche

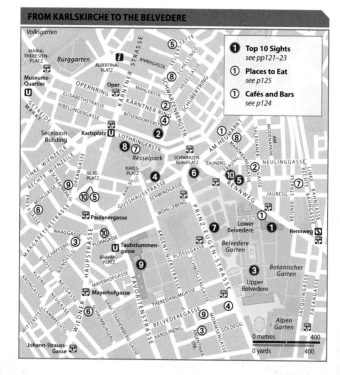

FROM KARLSKIRCHE TO THE BELVEDERE

> **1** Top 10 Sights
> *see pp121–23*
>
> **①** Places to Eat
> *see p125*
>
> **①** Cafés and Bars
> *see p124*

0 metres 400
0 yards 400

1 Salesianerinnenkirche
MAP F6 ■ Rennweg 8–10
■ **Closed to the public except during services 7am Mon–Sat, 9am Sun**

Amalia Wilhelmina (1673–1742), the wife of Emperor Joseph I, founded this monastery of the Salesian order in 1717 in thanks for her recovery from smallpox. The architect Donato Felice d'Allio completed the complex with its eight courtyards in 1728 and, together with the Belvedere and Palais Schwarzenberg, it forms a magnificent Baroque ensemble. The dome is decorated with frescoes by the Rococo painter Antonio Pellegrini (1675–1741) showing the Virgin Mary's ascension to heaven. According to Amalia Wilhelmina's will, her body is buried under the high altar, but an urn with her heart was placed inside her husband's coffin in the imperial crypt on Neuer Markt.

2 Musikverein
MAP N6 ■ Bösendorferstrasse 12 ■ Call 01 505 81 90 in advance for guided tours ■ Adm ■ www. musikverein.at

This impressive concert hall in Greek Renaissance style was built by Theophil von Hansen in 1869 for the Society of Friends of Music. It became famous after the Vienna Philharmonic Orchestra began giving their annual

Inside the Musikverein's Golden Hall

New Year's Concert here in 1941. There are three performance areas, but the main auditorium, the Golden Hall, is the finest, with lavish decorations and great acoustics (see p72).

3 The Belvedere
These two 18th-century palace buildings are linked by landscaped gardens, featuring tiered fountains and cascades, with statues of nymphs (see pp28–31).

4 Karlskirche
This Baroque masterpiece is one of Vienna's most impressive churches, with its beautiful carved columns and green dome (see pp32–3).

Karlskirche exterior

OTTO WAGNER

Before Otto Wagner (1841–1918) became one of Vienna's most eminent architects and an advocate of functional architecture, he was a Classical Revivalist. He moved from the Neo-Renaissance style to modernity by rejecting brick for steel structures. No other architect has left such a strong imprint on the city.

5 Gardekirche
MAP F5 ■ Rennweg 5a

The construction of this Rococo church was decreed by Empress Maria Theresa in 1755, and her favourite architect Nikolaus von Pacassi (1716–90) completed the building in 1763. The plain, cubic structure with a red tiled roof and a green cupola was the church to the nearby military hospital. The interior is decorated with elaborate stucco work, and behind the high altar is the painting *Christ on the Crucifix* by Peter Strudel, the founder of Vienna's first art school. The church has been the Polish national church in Vienna since 1897.

6 Liberation Monument
MAP F5 ■ Schwarzenbergplatz

This monument to the Soviet Red Army is a reminder of

Vienna's postwar history, when the city was occupied by the four Allied powers and divided into four zones. Schwarzenbergplatz was part of the Soviet zone and renamed Stalinplatz. The monument was installed in 1945 and, at the end of Allied occupation in 1955, the republic pledged to keep and maintain the monument.

7 Schwarzenberggarten
MAP F5 ■ Schwarzenbergplatz 9
■ Closed to the public

In 1697, the noted Baroque architect Lukas von Hildebrandt was commissioned to build a summer palace here, which was purchased by the influential Schwarzenberg family in 1720. Architects Johann Bernhard Fischer von Erlach and his son Josef Emanuel continued adorning the palace and laid out the garden in formal French style.

8 Otto Wagner Pavilion
MAP F4 ■ Karlsplatz
■ Exhibition: Open Apr–Oct: 10am–6pm Tue–Sun & public hols
■ Adm (free for under 19s)

The two pavilions on Karlsplatz were built by Otto Wagner in 1897 as twin stations for the Vienna City Train, the horse-drawn and then steam-powered predecessors of today's underground rail system. In total, Wagner designed 34 stations and various bridges and viaducts

Liberation Monument

Inside the Otto Wagner Pavilion

A DAY'S WALK FROM KARLSPLATZ TO THE BELVEDERE

for the train line that was finished in 1901. The pavilions on Karlsplatz are made of steel and marble slabs, and the roof over the arched gate is decorated with golden ornaments. Both stations became obsolete once the modern underground lines had been built. Today the Otto Wagner Pavilion is used by the Wien Museum and the other station is a café (see p124).

9 Theresianum
MAP G4 ■ Favoritenstrasse 15
■ Closed to the public

On the site of this elite private school once stood an imperial summer palace, until it was destroyed by Turkish troops in 1683. On its ruins the Italian architect Lodovico Burnacini built the Theresianum (1687–90). Comprising a long building with a sober façade, it was named after Empress Maria Theresa, who installed an educational institute here for the young nobility. Today it is a top private school and a diplomatic academy.

10 Palais Hoyos
MAP F5 ■ Rennweg 3 ■ Closed to the public

The renowned Otto Wagner built this Neo-Renaissance palace as his home in 1891, before he joined the Vienna Secessionist movement. The windows of the upper floor are framed with floral details, but the ground and first floors are built in sombre pale stone.

▶ MORNING

Start your day at Karlsplatz, where you can inspect the **Otto Wagner Pavilion** in Resselpark and then walk on to the splendid **Karlskirche** (see pp32–3). Left of the church is the **Wien Museum Karlsplatz** (see p57), where you could easily spend a few hours studying the city's history. Don't miss the Klimt and Schiele paintings, as well as Adolf Loos's original living room from 1903.

Head towards Argentinierstrasse, right of Karlskirche as you face away from the church, where you can enjoy some coffee and cake in **Café Goldegg** (see p124).

Walk east to the **Liberation Monument**, then take Rennweg and pass by Otto Wagner's **Palais Hoyos**. For lunch, pop into **Salm Bräu** (see p124).

AFTERNOON

It is now time to head for the **Belvedere** (see pp28–31), where you could easily spend the rest of the day. After having a look around the exhibition in the Lower Belvedere, walk through the formal gardens towards the Upper Belvedere, home to the Austrian National Gallery with many Klimt, Schiele, Gerstl and Amerssee paintings. You can also visit the 21er Haus gallery, located about ten minutes' walk from here on Arsenalstrasse 1. It holds changing exhibitions of Austrian art from 1945 to the present day.

Consider attending a concert in the **Konzerthaus** (see p73), but you need to book a day in advance.

See map on p120 ←

Cafés and Bars

Traditional dining area of Salm Bräu

1 Salm Bräu
MAP F5 ■ Rennweg 8
You not only get hearty dishes at Salm Bräu, but they also brew their own beers. The food complements the ale – make sure you try different sausage specialities and bread with various options.

2 Café Schwarzenberg
MAP N6 ■ Kärntner Ring 17
This is a traditional Viennese café with dark-wood interior, high ceilings, chandeliers, and period mirrors on the walls. In the summer, seating is on a terrace facing the Ringstrasse. The café hosts changing exhibitions of Viennese artists and there are piano concerts on Wednesday and Friday evenings (7:30–10pm).

3 Café Goldegg
MAP H5 ■ Argentinierstrasse 49/corner of Goldeggasse
A peaceful café and a retreat for reading the daily papers, Goldegg also has a games room where you can play chess or cards.

4 Café Imperial
MAP N6 ■ Kärntner Ring 16
This historic café opened in 1873 for the Universal Exhibition and is based in the former residence of the Prince of Württemberg. Enjoy a cup of coffee and one of the cafés signature tortes, whilst you soak up the opulent atmosphere.

5 Silver Bar at the Hotel Das Triest
MAP F4 ■ Wiedner Hauptstrasse 12
With its cool, laid-back vibe and first-class cocktails, the Silver Bar has long been the choice of Vienna's hip crowd. Enjoy a relaxed drink in its opulent surroundings.

6 Café Wortner
MAP G4 ■ Wiedner Hauptstrasse 55
A great historic coffee house with a whiff of the Biedermeier era about it; it's especially good for sitting outside.

7 Café Karl-Otto
MAP F4 ■ Otto Wagner Pavilion, Karlsplatz
Karl-Otto is a popular café/restaurant serving traditional food by day, and a club with international DJs by night.

8 Flanagan's Irish Pub
MAP N5 ■ Schwarzenberg-strasse 1–3
Enjoy pints of Guinness in a traditional Irish pub setting. The furniture was imported from a pub in Cork.

9 Point of Sale
MAP F4 ■ Schleifmühlgasse 12
This modern designer café serves all kinds of international breakfasts until late into the afternoon.

10 Artner auf der Wieden
MAP G4 ■ Floragasse 6
A cosy wine bar and restaurant. Try the homemade goat's cheese marinated in olive oil and herbs. You can also take a bottle home with you from the wine boutique.

See map on p120

Places to Eat

PRICE CATEGORIES

For a three-course meal for one with half
a bottle of wine (or equivalent meal),
taxes and extra charges.

€ under €35   €€ €35–70   €€€ over €70

1 Weinzirl

MAP P6 ▪ Am Heumarkt 6 ▪ 01
512 55 50 ▪ €€

Dine in the magnificent Art Nouveau
Konzerthaus. A delicious tapas lunch
is also served *(see p77)*.

2 Santa Lucia

MAP F6 ▪ Salesianergasse 10
▪ 01 714 21 63 ▪ €€

Vienna's only Italian/Indian eatery is
a favourite with locals. There's free
tiramisu with every dinner.

3 Wieden Bräu

MAP G4 ▪ Waaggasse 5 ▪ 01
586 03 00 ▪ €

This place serves Viennese food and
has a brewery, offering tours, that produces its own beer on the premises.

4 Art Corner

MAP G5 ▪ Prinz-Eugen-Straße
56/1 ▪ 01 505 18 21 ▪ €€

Despite being located so close to The
Belvedere, this Greek restaurant has
an authentic vibe. The owner will
give you a warm welcome.

5 Ribs of Vienna

MAP N4 ▪ Weihburggasse 22
▪ 01 513 85 19 ▪ €€

In a narrow room with bench tables in
a vaulted basement dating to 1591,
try the popular "one-metre spareribs".

6 Gasthaus Ubl

MAP F3 ▪ Pressgasse 26 ▪ 01
587 64 37 ▪ Closed Mon & Tue ▪ No
credit cards ▪ €

Probably Vienna's last simply styled
gasthaus is the perfect place for
dinner. Classic Viennese food is
served in oak-panelled surroundings.

7 Zur Steirischen Botschaft

MAP F6 ▪ Strohgasse 11 ▪ 01 712 33
67 ▪ Closed Sat & Sun in winter ▪ €

Dishes from Austria's southern
province of Styria are served in this
restaurant with a lovely garden.

8 Gmoa Keller

MAP P6 ▪ Am Heumarkt 25
▪ 01 712 53 10 ▪ Closed Sun & public
hols ▪ €

Favoured by musicians from the
concert halls nearby, this place
is known for its seasonal dishes
and wines.

9 Restaurant Sperl

MAP G5 ▪ Karolinengasse 13
▪ 01 504 73 34 ▪ €

Not to be confused with the famous
café of the same name *(see p118)*,
Sperl has an extensive menu of
Viennese and Austrian specialities.

10 Collio

MAP F4 ▪ Wiedner Hauptstrasse
12 ▪ 01 589 18 ▪ Closed Sun ▪ €€€

Fine Italian cooking is served in an
elegant setting at the Hotel Das
Triest *(see p142)*.

Collio's smart dining room

TOP 10 Greater Vienna

Horse heads on the wall of Hermesvilla stables

The city of Vienna is located where the hills of the Vienna Woods slope down into the Wiener Becken (the Vienna basin); from here the city spreads out on both sides of the Danube. The woods provide a welcome green belt and a recreation area for city dwellers. Today's suburbs, such as Grinzing and Nussdorf, were once countryside villages, until the city swallowed them up. In the 17th and 18th centuries the city's noble families built their summer residences within easy reach of the capital, but far enough out to benefit from cool rural surroundings during the hottest time of the year. Schloss Schönbrunn, Geymüllerschlössel and Hermesvilla were such examples. Also away from the centre, for reasons of hygiene and space, is the country's largest cemetery, the Zentralfriedhof.

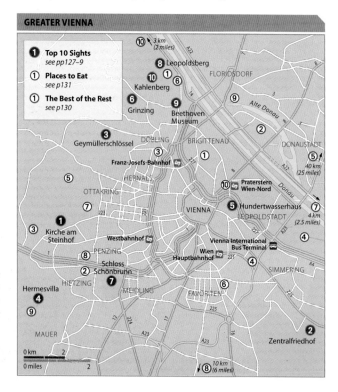

GREATER VIENNA

1 **Top 10 Sights**
see pp127–9

1 **Places to Eat**
see p131

1 **The Best of the Rest**
see p130

3 km (2 miles)

Leopoldsberg

FLORIDSDORF

Kahlenberg

Grinzing

Beethoven Museum

Alte Donau

Geymüllerschlössel   DÖBLING   BRIGITTENAU   DONAUSTADT

Franz-Josefs-Bahnhof

40 km (25 miles)

HERNALS

Praterstern Wien-Nord

OTTAKRING

VIENNA   LEOPOLDSTADT

Hundertwasserhaus

4 km (2.5 miles)

Kirche am Steinhof

Westbahnhof

Vienna International Bus Terminal

PENZING

Wien Hauptbahnhof

Schloss Schönbrunn

SIMMERING

Hermesvilla   HIETZING   MEIDLING   FAVORITEN

Zentralfriedhof

MAUER

0 km   2
0 miles   2

10 km (6 miles)

Detail from the exterior of the Art Nouveau Kirche am Steinhof

1 Kirche am Steinhof

Baumgartner Höhe 1 ■ Bus 47A, 48A ■ 01 910 60 11 007 ■ Open 4–5pm Sat, noon–4pm Sun ■ Guided tours: 3pm Sat, 4pm Sun & by appt ■ Adm

This church (see p55), another masterpiece by Otto Wagner (see p122), was created between 1905 and 1907 as a place of worship for the patients at the Steinhof psychiatric hospital. The hospital complex at the edge of the Vienna Woods was designed to bring patients closer to a healthy and natural environment so to help their recovery. Its golden dome can be seen from the Gloriette building in Schönbrunn Park.

2 Zentralfriedhof

Simmeringer Hauptstrasse 234, Tor 2 ■ Tram 71 ■ Open dawn–dusk

More than three million people have been buried in this 2.5-ha (6-acre) cemetery since it opened in 1874, among them 500 Austrian politicians, composers and actors. Max Hegele, Otto Wagner's student, designed the entrance portal, the mortuary and the Dr-Karl-Lueger-Gedächtniskirche, named after a Vienna mayor (1897–1910). The church is among Vienna's most important Art Nouveau buildings. Within the Zentralfriedhof are separate areas for followers of the Jewish, Islamic, Orthodox and Protestant faiths.

3 Geymüllerschlössel

Khevenmüllerstrasse 2 ■ Open May–Nov: 11am–6pm Sun ■ Tram 41 then Bus 41A ■ 711 36 298 ■ Adm

The Geymüllerschlössel is a summer palace off the beaten track, reflecting the Biedermeier style. Owned by the Museum of Applied Arts, it houses a collection of 170 clocks, among them an early Viennese flute clock (c.1800) that plays music by Haydn.

4 Hermesvilla

Lainzer Tiergarten ■ Bus 60B to Lainzer Tor and a 15-min walk; U-Bahn U4 and a 2-hr walk ■ Open Apr–Oct: 10am–6pm Tue–Sun & public hols ■ Adm ■ www.wienmuseum.at

Emperor Franz Joseph had this little palace built for his wife Elisabeth between 1882 and 1886 by architect Karl von Hasenauer and the imperial couple used to spend May and June here each year. The Hermes statue in the park gives the villa its name.

The pretty Hermesvilla palace

The colourful Hundertwasserhaus

5 Hundertwasserhaus

With perhaps the most unusual and colourful private residences in the world, this apartment block was built in 1985 by artist Friedensreich Hundertwasser (see pp40–41).

6 Grinzing
U-Bahn U4, U6; tram 38

Vienna is the only capital in the world where wine grapes are grown within the city boundaries – some 675 ha (1,670 acres) of vineyards are found here. The most widely known wine-growing community in the city is Grinzing. Once a small vintners' village on the outskirts of the city, it is today a hub of *heurigen*, with crowds of both locals and tourists flocking to the wine taverns (see pp80–81). The narrow streets still boast an old-fashioned rural charm.

7 Schloss Schönbrunn

This imperial Baroque palace, with its stunning landscaped gardens, is one of Vienna's most spectacular and most visited sights (see pp42–5).

8 Leopoldsberg
Train Nussdorf; bus 38A; U-Bahn U4 Heiligenstadt

Dominating the Danube valley is the the Leopoldsberg mountain. From its peak at 425 m (1,400 ft), you get an excellent view of the entire region around Vienna. Leopoldsberg is named after the Babenberg ruler Leopold III (1073–1136) and the ruins of the 13th-century Babenberg castle destroyed by the Turks in 1529 are still visible. An older church on top of the mountain was also destroyed by the Turks and was replaced by a Baroque church in the 18th century. Next to Leopoldsberg is its slightly higher twin peak, Kahlenberg.

VIENNA WOODS

The Vienna Woods spread towards the west of the city and were turned into a protected area as early as 1467 by Emperor Friedrich III. Then the forest was not endangered by road building but by people collecting firewood. In the 19th century, the forest was threatened with being cut down in a bid to gain resources, but today the Vienna Woods are as popular for excursions as ever.

---

9 Beethoven Museum
Probusgasse 6 ▪ U-Bahn U4, U6; tram D; Bus 38A ▪ Open 10am–6pm Tue–Sun ▪ Adm (free for under 19s and every first Sun)

In 2017, this small house where composer Ludwig van Beethoven lived during the summer was expanded by the Wien Museum and inaugurated as the first full-scale Beethoven Museum in Vienna. The famous composer came to the

then-rural village of Heligenstäder for its healing mineral springs to gain relief for his deafness. Unfortunately nothing helped. In 1802, while he was still here, he wrote the Heiligenstädter Testament, a poignant letter to his brothers. The letter was, however, never sent.

View over the Danube to Kahlenberg

⑩ Kahlenberg
Train Nussdorf; bus 38A

Covered with trees and vineyards, the 484-m- (1,580-ft-) high Kahlenberg mountain is on the edge of the Vienna Woods. The Höhenstrasse, a scenic route lined with trees, occasionally offers a glimpse of the city. It winds its way up from Grinzing, and the peak offers a breathtaking view of Vienna. During the Turkish siege of 1683, the Polish troops under King Jan III Sobieski descended from the top of this hill to defeat the Turkish army on 12 September that year. The little Baroque church on top of Kahlenberg commemorates this historic event.

Stunning façade of Schloss Schönbrunn

A DAY ON VIENNA'S OUTSKIRTS

 MORNING

To beat the crowds and enjoy the peace, begin your day at the magnificent former imperial summer residence **Schloss Schönbrunn** (see pp42–5). You could easily spend a day in the palace, walking in the park and the formal French garden, or visiting the world's oldest zoo at Schönbrunn Park. For a relaxing drink and a great view of the palace and the city, head to the far end of the park to the coffee house in the Gloriette building.

Stroll through the park towards the Hietzinger gate of the palace. Just around the corner is the Hietzinger Bräu, where you can get a taste of a real *tafelspitz* (see p74) for lunch.

AFTERNOON

After lunch, head to the **Kirche am Steinhof** (see p127). Take the U4 Schönbrunn U-bahn to the Unter St Veit stop, then cross the street to reach the 47A bus stop. Take the bus from here. It will pass Baumgarten cemetery en route to the Otto Wagner Hospital. From here a wooded path winds up to the church.

From Kirche am Steinhof opt to head to the leafy *heuringen* of Grinzing for a relaxing evening.

Walk north from the church on the footpath to **Pönningerweg**. From here the 46A bus takes you to **Ottakring station**. Next, take the S45 Schnellbahn train to **Wien Oberdöbling Bahnhof**, from where the 38 tram goes straight to **Grinzing**.

See map on p126 ←

The Best of the Rest

1 Nussdorf
Train Nussdorf; tram D

Nussdorf's picturesque location amid hills overgrown with vineyards is complemented by its long narrow streets.

2 Vienna International Centre
Wagramerstrasse 5 ▪ U-Bahn U1 ▪ Guided tours (ID needed) 11am & 2pm Mon–Fri (Jul–Aug: also 12:30pm) ▪ Adm ▪ www.unvienna.org

This centre, also known as the UNO City, dominates the skyline. Built in the 1970s, the building is the Vienna headquarters of the United Nations.

3 Ernst Fuchs Museum
Hüttelbergstrasse 26 ▪ U-Bahn U4; bus 52A, 52B ▪ Open 10am–4pm Tue–Sun & by special appt (call 01 914 85 75) ▪ Adm ▪ www. ernstfuchsmuseum.at

A stunning villa, built by Otto Wagner but altered later by Ernst Fuchs, whose paintings are displayed here alongside Wagner's memorabilia.

4 Sankt-Marxer-Friedhof
Leberstrasse 6–8 ▪ Bus 74A ▪ Open daily

The St Marx Cemetery is the resting place for prominent Austrians, including Mozart, whose actual burial site remains shrouded in mystery.

5 Schloss Hof
Imperial Festival Palace Hof ▪ Open Apr–Oct: 10am–6pm daily ▪ www.schlosshof.at

This was the former country seat of Prince Eugene of Savoy and later Empress Maria Theresa.

6 Lehár-Schikaneder Schlössl
Hackhofergasse 18 ▪ U-Bahn U4; tram D ▪ Open by appt (call 01 318 5416)

This Baroque palace was once home to Emanuel Schikaneder, who wrote the libretto for *The Magic Flute*, and later to composer Franz Lehár.

7 Lobau
U-Bahn U1; bus 92B, 93A

Spread over more than 4,900 acres (1,983 ha), the Lobau is wild national parkland, locally known as "Vienna's jungle", featuring lakes, secluded forest and wildlife.

8 Laxenburg
U-Bahn U1, then bus from Südtiroler Platz ▪ www.schloss-laxenburg.at

The Laxenburg palace and its park were established by Empress Maria Theresa in the 18th century.

9 Lainer Tiergarten
1130 Vienna ▪ U-Bahn Hütteldorf ▪ Open 8am–dusk daily ▪ www.lainzer-tiergarten.at

This former hunting area, with sheltered observation areas and walkways, is now a wildlife refuge with wild boar, deer and bighorn sheep.

10 Klosterneuburg
U-Bahn U4; bus 238, 239; train Klosterneuburg

This ancient town has a fine Augustine abbey founded in the early 12th century by Babenberg ruler Leopold III.

Schloss Hof palace

Places to Eat

PRICE CATEGORIES

For a three-course meal for one with half a bottle of wine (or equivalent meal), taxes and extra charges.

€ under €35 ■ €€ €35–70 ■ €€€ over €70

① Mraz & Sohn
Wallensteinstrasse 59 ■ Tram 5, 33 ■ 01 330 45 94 ■ €€€

This restaurant is simply one of the best in Vienna. The chef's innovative cooking can be enjoyed in a relaxed and inviting minimalist setting.

② Café Dommayer
Johann-Strauss-Platz/ Auhofstrasse 2 ■ U-Bahn U4 ■ 01 877 54 65 ■ €

Dommayer is a traditional café with red velvet upholstery, a wooden veranda and a pretty garden. Johann Strauss used to give concerts here.

③ Fischer Bräu
Billrothstrasse 17 ■ U-Bahn U6; tram 37, 38 ■ 01 369 59 49 ■ No credit cards ■ €

There is a great atmosphere in this restaurant and pub, with its old wooden interior and own brewery. The beer garden is pleasant in summer.

④ Café-Restaurant Lusthaus
Freudenau 254, end of Prater Hauptallee ■ Bus 77A ■ 01 728 95 65 ■ €€

This octagonal pavilion in the middle of the Prater park was built in 1874 as a meeting point for the imperial hunting party. It is now a charming restaurant with windows on all sides offering lovely views of the park.

⑤ Villa Aurora
Wilhelminenstrasse 237 ■ Bus 146 ■ 01 489 33 33 ■ No credit cards ■ €€

In a spectacular location overlooking the city, Villa Aurora serves inventive schnitzel creations and vegetarian dishes. There is a garden for picnics.

⑥ Meixner's Gastwirtschaft
Buchengasse 64 ■ U-Bahn U1 ■ 01 604 27 10 ■ Closed Sat & Sun ■ €€

Family-owned Meixner's prepares Viennese cuisine at the highest level. Be sure to sample the Austrian lamb.

Meixner's Gastwirtschaft's courtyard

⑦ Plachutta Grünspan
Ottakringer Strasse 266 ■ U-Bahn U3; bus 45B, 46B; tram 46 ■ 01 480 57 30 ■ No credit cards ■ €€

Vienna's most acclaimed beer garden, with indoor seating all year round.

⑧ Hadikstüberl
Hadikgasse 100 ■ U-Bahn U4 ■ 01 894 63 21 ■ Closed Sun ■ No credit cards ■ €€

A genuine Viennese restaurant with a rustic interior. Dishes vary seasonally.

⑨ La Creperie
An der Oberen Alten Donau 6 ■ U-Bahn U6 ■ 01 270 31 00 ■ €€

Open until midnight, this creperie is frequented by tourists and locals alike.

⑩ Tempel
MAP B6 ■ Praterstrasse 56, inner courtyard ■ U-Bahn Nestroyplatz ■ 01 214 01 79 ■ Closed Sun ■ €€

Near the house where the *Blue Danube Waltz* was penned, Tempel offers inexpensive lunch menus.

See map on p126

Streetsmart

Exterior of the Hundertwasserhaus

Exterior of the Hundertwasserhaus

Getting To and Around Vienna

Arriving by Air

Vienna International Airport, known locally as Schwechat, serves over 100 airlines, including budget carriers, and is the flight hub of Austrian Airlines. Taxis will take passengers to any destination in the centre for a fixed €36. Buses from Vienna Airport Lines go to all major areas for €8 (under 14s free). A non-stop City Airport Train called **CAT** offers luxury seating and a 16-minute ride to Wien Mitte train station for €11. A faster and cheaper alternative is the new Railjet high-speed train, which takes 15 minutes and costs €3.90, stopping at the main Hauptbahnhof railway station.

Arriving by Train

The **Austrian Federal Railways** (or ÖBB) has, in recent years, introduced new sophisticated trains. The 230 km/h (143 mph) Railjet has free access to movies and Wi-Fi. There are also electrical charging stations for laptops. Since its opening in 2014, the rebuilt **Hauptbahnhof** (Central Station) has seen a rerouting of train lines for greater efficiency. The Hauptbahnhof, signposted sometimes just as Wien HBF, is the nation's hub, but not the most central station in the city, being off to the southeast. Wien Mitte, by contrast, is within walking distance of the Stephansdom, and is the hub of the airport shuttle CAT.

Arriving by Coach

With the advent of cheap airfares, coach travel is less popular. **Eurolines** is a consortium of 30 companies, with offices at **VIB**, or Vienna International Busterminal Edberg, close to the main railway station. Once in the city, there are excellent bus links with the rest of the country.

Arriving by Car

All drivers must carry a first-aid kit, a warning triangle, a high-visibility vest and – on designated mountain roads – snow chains in winter. Drivers must be at least 18, and children under 12 must sit at the back. Non-EU citizens (including those from North America and Australia) must have an international driving licence. Every car driving on motorways must display a *vignette* toll sticker, bought at any petrol station. Penalties for unpaid tolls are high. Speed limits are 50 km/h (30 mph) within all towns and villages, 100 km/h (60 mph) on country roads and 130 km/h (80 mph) on motorways.

Arriving by Boat

A high-speed hydrofoil service run by **Twin City Liner** links Vienna to cities along the Danube, including Bratislava, Passau and Budapest. It is a 75-minute journey to Bratislava in a 109-seater air-conditioned catamaran that also has a full on-board buffet. Dogs and bicycles are allowed.

Arriving by Bicycle

Two-wheeling visitors can arrive in Vienna on the **Danube Cycle Path**, with its pretty villages, gardens and fairytale spires. This impressive cycleway follows the Danube River for 900 km (560 miles) and is home to a collection of "Bed+Bike" accommodation that is certified cycle-friendly and found in around 50 different locations between Vienna and Passau. Around 40 suggested cycling tours branch off the main path. Austria has embraced the e-bike so the route has charging stations and e-bike facilities.

Travelling by Public Transport

A joined-up transit system run by **Wiener Linien** accepts interchangeable tickets across its buses, trams and train services. The best value are tickets that are valid for 24 hours (€7.60), 48 hours (€13.30), 72 hours (€16.50) and for unlimited travel from 8am until 8pm (€6.10). A single ticket costs €2.20 (€2.30 if bought on board) with reduced (€1.20) tickets for children, dogs and bikes. To avoid a fine, validate your ticket at the blue machines at the underground station entrance or on buses and trams.

Use **AnachB** (meaning A-to-B) to plan journeys by public transport, car, bicycle or on foot.

There are 127 numbered bus routes forming the city's bus network, the only public transport system that serves the central 1st district as well as some suburbs. Tickets are purchased or validated on board the bus. The ÖBB intercity bus service has excellent links with the rest of Austria.

Trams have been part of Vienna's transit system since 1865, when vehicles were horse-drawn. Today, a large network serves the city: look at the front of the tram for the destination and buy or validate a ticket on board. Many trams are street-level models for easy access.

Vienna's metro system consists of five lines, with a sixth under construction. Five stations were added to the main U1 line in 2017, making a total of 109 stations. Each station is also a hub for buses and trams.

Travelling by Car

Several car hire firms operate in Vienna, from international rental companies to national and local hire options. Look for booths at the airport, or pre-book online.

Travelling by Taxi

Taxis are plentiful and charge a €3.80 minimum fee (during the day) plus €0.20 per kilometre. At night, on Sundays or on public holidays, the minimum charge is €4.30. Phone to book or hail at a taxi stand – for Vienna-wide locations see the **Vienna Taxis** section on the government website or download a free Vienna taxi app. Smartphone taxis now operating in Vienna include Uber, MyDriver and Blacklane.

Travelling by Boat

The boarding station for most Danube boat journeys is on a tributary at Schwedenplatz or at the Reichsbrücke on the river. The biggest operator is **DDSG Blue Danube**.

Travelling by Horse-Drawn Carriage

Old-fashioned horsepower is behind Vienna's most leisurely mode of transport, a traditional horse-pulled *fiaker* (taxi). Pre-book or get one at the official ranks at the Staatsoper, Hofburg or Stephansdom.

Travelling by Bicycle

Getting around by bicycle is cheap and easy thanks to the **CityBike Vienna** rental service. Register online or at a CityBike Terminal with a credit card. The first hour is free, after which a sliding-scale fee applies depending on duration (€1–€4 per hour). There are 120 CityBike stations in the city. Many companies run guided cycle tours *(see p139)*. A cycling map is available at tourist information points. Man-powered pedicabs offer quick and inexpensive short trips from stations to hotels or sights.

Travelling on Foot

Compared to many cities, Vienna's size means it's easily navigable on foot. Pedestrian areas and cobbled backstreets are waiting to be discovered in the corners of the historic Ringstrasse. Some tour companies run themed walks *(see p139)*.

(see p139)

DIRECTORY

ARRIVING BY AIR

CAT
🆆 cityairporttrain.com

Vienna International Airport
🆆 viennaairport.com

ARRIVING BY TRAIN

Austrian Federal Railways
🆆 oebb.at/en

Hauptbahnhof
🆆 hauptbahn-wien.at

ARRIVING BY COACH

Eurolines
🆆 eurolines.at

VIB
🆆 buslinien.at/en

ARRIVING BY BOAT

Twin City Liner
🆆 twincityliner.com

ARRIVING BY BICYCLE

Danube Cycle Path
🆆 danube-cycle-path.com

TRAVELLING BY PUBLIC TRANSPORT

AnachB
🆆 anachb.at

Wiener Linien
🆆 wienerlinien.at

TRAVELLING BY TAXI

Vienna Taxis
🆆 wien.gv.at/stadtplan/en/

TRAVELLING BY BOAT

DDSG Blue Danube
🆆 ddsg-blue-danube.at

TRAVELLING BY BICYCLE

CityBike Vienna
🆆 citybikewien.at

Practical Information

Passports and Visas

Visitors from outside the European Economic Area (EEA), European Union (EU) and Switzerland need a valid passport to travel to Austria, as do UK visitors. Swiss, EEA and EU nationals can use identity cards instead. Visitors from Canada, the US, Australia and New Zealand can stay for up to 30 days without a visa, as long as their passport is valid for 6 months beyond the date of entry. A visa is necessary for longer stays and must be obtained in advance from the Austrian embassy (Schengen visas are valid). All other visitors need valid passports and visas. Check the **Austrian Foreign Ministry** website for details.

Most countries have consular representation in Vienna, including the **US**, **Canada**, **Australia**, **New Zealand** and the **UK**.

Customs and Immigration

For EU citizens, there are no restrictions on importing cigarettes, spirits and perfume as long as they are for personal use. From outside the EU, you can import 200 cigarettes, 1 litre of spirits, 4 litres of wine and up to €175 in other goods duty free. Cash over €10,000 taken into or out of the EU must be declared.

Travel Safety Advice

Visitors can get up-to-date travel safety information from the **UK Foreign and Commonwealth Office**, the **US Department of State** and the **Australian Department of Foreign Affairs and Trade**.

Travel Insurance

All travellers are advised to buy travel insurance. Dental care is not covered and prescriptions and some medical bills may need to be paid upfront and claimed back later – check your policy. EU citizens need to carry a valid **EHIC** (European Health Insurance Card) to get free or low-cost emergency medical treatment.

Health

Austria has a fine health care system that offers first-class medical treatment. Doctors and medical staff speak good English. Waiting times in surgeries and emergency rooms in Vienna are also surprisingly short. Several organizations run ambulance services across the city. If you need an out-of-hours doctor, call the **Emergency Doctor Service**.

Dental surgeries are open for standard as well as night and weekend services. For out-of-hours help, call the **Emergency Dental Service** (recorded information).

Pharmacies (apotheken) have a green cross and red "A" outside. Find them in the telephone directory or call the **Emergency Chemist Service** (German recorded information) from 8am to 6pm Monday to Friday and from 8am to midday on Saturday.

Personal Security

Vienna is one of Europe's safer capitals, with fairly low levels of petty crime. However, visitors should remain alert for incidents of pickpocketing and distraction thefts at ATMs. Carry little of value and keep cash and phones out of sight. The police maintain a strong presence and there is a low tolerance of law-breaking. As well as taking the usual precautions, avoid the Prater theme park in winter when it is deserted. Underground stations such as Praterstern and Meidling are also best avoided after dark.

Emergency Services

Ambulance, **police** and **fire** services can be called for free. **All emergency services** can also be reached by dialling the pan-European emergency number. Insurance companies require police reports for any claims. Police must be called for any accident involving injury.

Travellers with Specific Needs

The official **Vienna Tourist Board** website has a vast resource that includes all accessible attractions, hotels, eateries and public conveniences, plus where to board accessible public transport. There are also lists of suppliers that hire out mobility aids and transport companies that provide special services for passengers who have hearing or other disabilities. Many older hotels lack access facilities, so the tourist board has nominated hotels suitable for people with specific needs. All tourist offices also have information booklets.

Many of the city's public buses are street-level vehicles with fold-out ramps. Most tram lines have street-level trams; look out for stops displaying a flashing wheelchair symbol and a minute-counter for when the next low-floor tram is due. Underground stations are equipped with "guiding stripes" to help visually impaired travellers navigate escalators, exits and lifts. A Braille station map of Vienna's underground system can be purchased

from the public transport operator **Wiener Linien** *(see p135).*

Many restaurants are wheelchair-accessible and offer disabled parking. Those in historic buildings are harder to access.

Several companies also offer services to visitors with disabilities, including **Bizeps**, the **Austrian Blind Union** and the **Austrian Association for the Hearing Impaired**.

Currency and Banking

Austria's official currency is the euro. Banknotes come in denominations of €5, €10, €20, €50, €100, €200 and €500 (the latter is rarely seen). Coins are 1c, 2c, 5c, 10c, 20c, 50c, €1 and €2. Visitors from

outside the eurozone should check exchange rates at the time of travel. Money can be changed at banks, bureaux de change or one of the automated changing machines found across the city.

Cash can be withdrawn at banks and about 3,000 cash machines (ATMs) throughout Austria – they are denoted by a sign with the letter "B" in blue and green. National and international Maestro cards (cash cards) and Visa, MasterCard and American Express credit cards are all accepted. International ATMs usually charge a fee when you use your credit or debit card – the amount will vary from bank to bank. Most shops and restaurants accept payment by debit card.

DIRECTORY

PASSPORTS AND VISAS

Australia
Mattiellistrasse 2-4
43 1 506 740 (not for visa enquiries)
austria.embassy.gov.au

Austrian Foreign Ministry
bmeia.gv.at/en/

Canada
Laurenzerberg 2
43 1 531 38 3000
austria.gc.ca

New Zealand
Mattiellistrasse 2-4
43 1 505 3021
mfat.govt.nz

UK
Jauresgasse 12
43 1 716130
ukinaustria.fco.gov.uk

US
Boltzmanngasse 16
43 1 313 390
at.usembassy.gov

TRAVEL SAFETY ADVICE

Australian Department of Foreign Affairs and Trade
dfat.gov.au
smartraveller.gov.au

UK Foreign and Commonwealth Office
gov.uk/foreign-travel-advice

US Department of State
travel.state.gov

TRAVEL INSURANCE

EHIC
nhs.uk/ehic

HEALTH

Emergency Chemist Service
1550

Emergency Dental Service
01 512 20 78

Emergency Doctor Service
141

EMERGENCY SERVICES

All Emergency Services
112

Ambulance
144

Fire
122

Police
133

TRAVELLERS WITH SPECIFIC NEEDS

Austrian Association for the Hearing Impaired
01 603 08 53
oeglb.at

Austrian Blind Union
01 982 7584-0
oebsv.at

Bizeps
01 523 8921
bizeps.or.at

Vienna Tourist Board
43 1 24 555
wien.info

Internet and Telephone

Vienna has more than 400 free internet hotspots, including train stations and many hotels. The **City of Vienna** website has a free interactive map showing the Wi-Fi hot spots. There's also a city map to help locate taxi stands and CityBike stations as well as venues with facilities for people with specific needs.

To phone Vienna from abroad dial the international prefix (00 from the UK and Europe, 011 from North America or 0011 from Australia), then dial Austria's country code (always 43) followed by Vienna's city code (1 for landlines and 6 for mobile lines), then the phone number. Unlike most countries, Austrian phone numbers do not have a fixed number of digits.

Visitors who are staying for extensive periods may find buying an inexpensive Austrian prepaid phone or SIM card worthwhile.

Postal Services

Austria's postal service, established in 1490, is the oldest standardized postal service in Europe. There are two mailing options from Austria to foreign destinations – priority and economy for Europe and the rest of the world. A standard letter (up to 20g) is automatically posted as priority and will reach the UK in a couple of days and the US in less than a week. Stamps are sold at all post offices. Red stripes on a yellow post box indicates that they are emptied on Sundays

and public holidays. Vienna's yellow-fronted post offices are open 8am–noon & 2–6pm Mon–Fri some stay open during lunch. Suboffices in railway stations are often open 24 hours daily. Find the locations and hours on the **Post** website.

Television and Radio

State broadcaster **ORF** runs ORF eins, ORF 2 and ORF III, and there are several private channels such as **ATV** and **Servus TV**. Most hotels offer satellite channels. Radio station **FM4** broadcasts news in English, German and French on 103.8. Radio station **Ö1** has news in English and French on weekdays at 12:50pm.

Newspapers and Magazines

Newsstands in Austria are dominated by state-subsidized publications that each have different party affiliations. The largest is the tabloid **Kronen Zeitung**, which has an upmarket sister, the **Kurier**. The most respected daily newspaper is **Die Presse**, with **Der Standard** the best for business and economics. Larger newsstands will sell international papers, usually one day after publication. **Falter** is the main listings magazine.

Opening Hours

Shops are usually open 9am–6:30pm Mon–Fri and 9am–5pm Sat; some shopping centres are open until 8pm or 9pm. In this predominantly Catholic country

most shops are closed on Sundays, other than in the larger railway stations, at the airport and in the museums.

Most banks are open 8am–12:30pm and 1:30–3pm Monday to Friday (to 5:30pm Friday). In the city centre (1st district) banks don't close for lunch.

Restaurants open daily in the city centre, with those in the outer districts closing for one or two days each week.

Museum opening times vary but most are open 10am–5pm, closing on either Monday or Tuesday. Some of the larger attractions stay open late one evening, often until 9pm.

Time Differences

Vienna is in the Central European Time (CET) zone, one hour ahead of Greenwich Mean Time (GMT). Austria switches to daylight saving time (CEST) from the last Sunday in March to the last Sunday in October.

Electrical Appliances

Vienna's standard mains voltage is 230 V. The standard frequency is 50 Hz. Electrical plugs have twin round pins. Devices from North America will need both a frequency adaptor and a voltage converter.

Driving

Non-EU citizens should carry a valid international driving licence at all times. If travelling outside of the city limits, you will also need to display a *vignette* (toll sticker) on motorways and A roads.

Weather

Vienna's biting winds can make winter (late October to March) feel much colder than a few degrees below zero. Summer in the city (June to end of August) tends to be warm and sunny, but July and August can be sweltering so make sure you book an air-conditioned room if staying in the old city.

Language

German is spoken in Austria, although Vienna has a specific dialect of Austro-Bavarian, containing many examples of unique vocabulary, that is considered quintessentially Austrian by the rest of the country. The most commonly spoken foreign language is English.

Smoking

Austria has one of the highest rates of smoking in Europe. Smoking has long been a part of café culture in Vienna and plans to introduce a total smoking ban in cafés and restaurants by 2018 were overturned in late 2017 . Currently most public places have separate non-smoking and smoking sections. It is illegal to smoke in a car with children present.

Visitor Information

Multilingual staff offer public transport information, free maps and leaflets about attractions and day trips at tourist offices. Main branches can be found in the arrivals hall at Vienna International Airport and the Information Point at Central Station as well as at Albertinaplatz/Maysedergasse, with pop-up visitor information booths scattered around the city centre.

Trips and Tours

There are seemingly unlimited ways to explore Vienna, from underground tunnels, city walks and night-time bar-hops to open-topped buses, cycle tours, Segway tours and horse-and-carriage rides.

Vienna Walks & Talks, **PerPedes** and **Wiener Spaziergänge** run fascinating historical walks led by highly knowledgeable guides that specialize in the arts, music, architecture and social history. They also run other thematic tours, including culinary and film tours.

A number of firms, such as **Segway & E-Fatbike in the City**, offer inventive ways of exploring the city, while **Red Bus City Tours** and **Vienna Sightseeing** are veterans of the city's vehicular sightseeing routes, with hop-on-hop-off tours also on offer. Two-wheeled excursions don't come better than **Pedal Power**, while boat cruises, trips and Danube exploration into neighbouring nations are a speciality of **DDSG Blue Danube** (see p135).

For a unique view of the city, follow in the footsteps of Orsen Welles, who as Harry Lime delved into the underworld of sewers for the filming of the epic cult movie, *The Third Man*; mysterious tours into the city's depths and around the city's other film locations are run in summer by **3. Mann Tour** (see p64).

(see p135)
(see p64)

DIRECTORY

INTERNET AND TELEPHONE

City of Vienna
🌐 wien.gv.at

POSTAL SERVICES

Post
🌐 post.at

TELEVISION AND RADIO

ATV
🌐 atv.at

FM4
103.8FM
🌐 fm4.orf.at

Ö1
91.9 FM
🌐 oe1.orf.at

ORF
🌐 orf.at

Servus TV
🌐 servustv.com

NEWSPAPERS AND MAGAZINES

Der Standard
🌐 derstandard.at

Die Presse
🌐 diepresse.com

Falter
🌐 falter.at

Kronen Zeitung
🌐 krone.at

Kurier
🌐 kurier.at

TRIPS AND TOURS

Pedal Power
🌐 pedalpower.at

PerPedes
🌐 perpedes.at

Red Bus City Tours
🌐 redbuscitytours.at

Segway & E-Fatbike in the City
🌐 segwayrentalvienna.com

Vienna Sightseeing
🌐 viennasightseeing.at

Vienna Walks & Talks
🌐 viennawalks.com

Wiener Spaziergänge
🌐 wienguide.at

Shopping

The city's mix of shopping streets, malls and pedestrian zones offers visitors a wide variety of fashion, local goods and souvenirs in a great array of jewellery shops, antique stores, art stores, boutiques, delicatessens, chocolate shops, wine cellars, high street chain stores and sports shops.

One of the newest additions to the Viennese shopping scene is the **Goldenes Quartier**, where exclusive brands such as Viviene Westwood, Louis Vuitton, Emporio Armani, Miu Miu, Roberto Cavalli, Prada and Saint Laurent vie for attention in swish air-conditioned premises located in the heart of the 1st district between Am Hof, Bognergasse and Tuchlauben, which lie next to the upmarket Kohlmarkt pedestrianized shopping street.

Away from the high-end shopping streets centred on the 1st district around the Kärntner Strasse, Graben and Kohlmarkt area are the less pricy options in Mariahilfer Strasse and Kärntner Strasse, where you'll find Zara, H&M and Esprit. Large shopping centres include **BahnhofCity Wien West** at Westbahnhof station and **The Mall** at Wien Mitte station, as well as the **Donauzentrum** (U1 line to Kagran) and the **Stadion Center** (U2 line to Stadion).

Throughout the city shoppers will find plenty of opportunities to snap up all kinds of chocolates, cakes and pastries. These include Vienna's world-famous chocolate tart,

Sachertorte. High-quality ground coffees and beans are sold everywhere, as is beautiful glassware and porcelain decorated with traditional Viennese patterns – **Augarten** offers buyers perhaps the finest examples. Other Austrian goods include warm coats and jackets made of the woollen fabric loden, as well as traditional dirndl dresses. Gift-wrapped schnapps, jams, pickled vegetables, special vinegars and cheese can be purchased at the busy **Naschmarkt** *(see p116)*.

For really exquisite Viennese jewellery visit the hallowed showrooms of **Köchert and Heldwein**, who were once jewellers to the imperial court. **Frey Wille** and **Österreichische Werkstätten** offer buyers a dazzling Art Nouveau-inspired range that is highly collectable. You will find more desirable artifacts and gilded treasures at **The Dorotheum**, which was established in 1707 by Emperor Joseph I and is one of the most important auction houses in the world. Approximately 600 auctions are held here each year, together with an extensive range of jewellery items at fixed prices. Vienna also hosts **WestLicht**, a twice-yearly auction of rare and valuable old cameras.

VAT (Value-Added Tax), also known as a Goods and Services Tax (GST), is levied at the rate of 20 per cent in Austria. All visitors coming in from non-EU countries are entitled to a VAT/GST refund on purchases that cost more than €75. Look out for the Global Refund Tax Free Shopping stickers in shop

windows or ask the store assistant for details. Ask for a tax refund form in any shop where you make purchases over €75 and fill out the form in its entirety. Keep receipts from all relevant sales and present them along with the forms at the airport. You will need a customs officer to stamp the forms and you can then take them to a bank or currency exchange office for a tax refund.

While credit cards are widely accepted they aren't welcomed everywhere in Vienna. Some small restaurants and shops only take cash and may also refuse to handle large denomination notes. Others may charge for accepting payment by credit card.

Sunday shopping isn't widespread in Vienna and most shops stay closed. However, supermarkets and bakeries are granted an exemption, together with shops at some train stations, airports, tourist locations and bigger fuel stations. Some large malls open for restricted shopping hours.

Dining

Vienna looks good, but tastes even better; the cuisine mixes flavours from across Austria with a hotchpotch of influences from the Habsburg lands of the imperial era. Individual dishes and cooking styles have been handpicked from each country and adapted to suit the Viennese palate. Bordering nations add to the culinary pot, as do recent immigrants – and while the Viennese love traditional hearty and meat-heavy dishes, there has been a shift in recent years to lighter meals. Most restaurants offer vegetarian dishes and the city has an incredible array of ethnic eateries.

Every other shop in the city seems to sell cakes and pastries accompanied by a cup of coffee, and there are also the usual fast-food joints, ice-cream parlours and a growing number of organic cafés and juice bars.

Vienna's much beloved *heurigen* (wine taverns) also serve inexpensive Austrian dishes, and local *würstelstände* are excellent for late-night cheap eats – you'll find one of these sizzling sausage stalls on virtually every street corner.

Dining out in Vienna can be a wonderful excuse to dress up if you're eating in one of the city's finest restaurants. Otherwise, casual attire is perfectly acceptable. Reservations are advisable if you plan to eat at one of the city's most celebrated restaurants – some are booked up weeks in advance.

The variety of eateries mirrors the variation in prices. A breakfast of roll, jam and coffee can cost as little as €5, and in a *beisl* (traditional Austrian inn) you may pay as little as €4.50 for a bowl of soup and around €12 for a main course. Lunch in a luxury restaurant will usually start at about €20. Most places offer a bargain midday set menu for a two- or three-course meal for around €13.

Vienna's cosy traditional coffee shops are a part of the city's charm, but if you have no time for a slow-paced cup of high-grade coffee you'll find several branches of Starbucks together with plenty of fast-food joints that will serve an average cup of coffee to go.

Tipping your server around 5 per cent is customary in Austria if the service has been good. To tip, simply hand over the cash and say *danke* (thank you), which implies they should keep the change.

Accommodation

Vienna's hotels offer an incredible variety of accommodation options, from self-catering apartments, *pensionen* (B&Bs) and starred hotels to rooms in private apartments, youth hostels and campsites. For those on a budget, some of the student halls of residence are rented out to tourists over the summer, and youth hostels offer communal dorm accommodation at shoestring rates. Alternatively, visitors can pitch a tent or camper van at one of Vienna's four well-appointed campsites.

Airbnb now lists over 5,000 properties in Vienna. A hotel's location has a huge bearing on the price, with Vienna's 1st district the most expensive. The further out you stay, the more inexpensive the hotels and B&Bs become, although the Town Hall and MuseumsQuartier area have some excellent budget accommodation close to the city centre. Costs usually include a continental breakfast in B&Bs and a buffet in some hotels. The price quoted will include VAT. The low season runs from January to March, when discounts are sometimes offered for longer, pre-paid stays. In peak season (from April to the end of December) you'll need to make sure you book in advance. Be sure to check out the booking service of the **Vienna Tourist Board** *(see p137)* and **Vienna Camping**.

(see p137)

DIRECTORY

SHOPPING

Augarten
W augarten.at

BahnhofCity Wien West
W bahnhofcitywienwest.at

Donauzentrum
W donauzentrum.at

Frey Wille
W www.freywille.com

Goldenes Quartier
W goldenesquartier.com

Köchert and Heldwein
W koechert.com

Österreichische Werkstätten
W oew.at

Stadion Center
W stadioncenter.at

The Dorotheum
W dorotheum.com

The Mall
W wienmitte-themall.at

WestLicht
W westlicht-auction.com

WHERE TO STAY

Airbnb
W airbnb.at

Vienna Camping
W wiencamping.at

Places to Stay

PRICE CATEGORIES
For a standard, double room per night (with breakfast if included), taxes and extra charges.

€ under €150 €€ €150–280 €€€ over €280

Luxury Hotels

Hotel Das Triest
MAP F4 ■ Wiedner Hauptstrasse 12 ■ 01 589 18 ■ www.dastriest. at ■ €€
This chic boutique hotel is located within walking distance of most of the major attractions. It has a pretty courtyard garden where you can dine in summer, and the rooms – some with their own terrace or direct garden access – are individually furnished and feature works by international and local artists.

Hotel de France
MAP L1 ■ Schottenring 3 ■ 01 313 680 ■ www. hoteldefrance.at ■ €€
Built in 1872, this hotel retains the elegant style of this era, which is now combined with modern comforts. Facilities at the hotel include conference and banqueting halls, and three restaurants.

Renaissance Wien Hotel
Linke Wienzeile/ Ullmanstrasse 71 ■ U-Bahn U4 ■ 01 891 02 ■ www.renaissancewien. at ■ €€
Part of the Marriott chain, the hotel is situated near Schloss Schönbrunn and is just ten minutes on the underground from the city centre sights. Alongside other facilities, there is an indoor rooftop pool.

DO & CO Hotel
MAP N3 ■ Stephansplatz 12 ■ 01 241 88 ■ www. docohotel.com ■ €€€
The DO & CO Hotel is an architectural landmark in the city. The curved glass exterior exudes superior design and advertises the standards of comfort inside. This place has all the amenities of a world-class hotel alongside an impeccable location at the cathedral. The restaurant is excellent (see p99).

Hotel Bristol
MAP N6 ■ Kärntner Ring 1 ■ 01 515 160 ■ www. bristolvienna.com ■ €€€
One of the top addresses in town, Hotel Bristol is where celebrities and politicians often stay for official or private visits. The 140 rooms offer great views of the Staatsoper opposite. The hotel provides you with all sorts of thoughtful treats, such as umbrellas for rainy days.

Hotel Sacher
MAP M5 ■ Philhar- monikerstrasse 4 ■ 01 514 56 ■ www.sacher.com ■ €€€
Ever since this hotel was founded in 1876 it has been a Viennese institu- tion, with guests ranging from emperors and diplo- mats to artists. At the café next door, writers such as Arthur Schnitzler used to enjoy the famous Sachertorte with a coffee. The hotel still ranks

among Vienna's most luxurious. All rooms are individually furnished.

Imperial
MAP N6 ■ Kärntner Ring 16 ■ 01 501 100 ■ www. imperialvienna.com ■ €€€
This grand hotel opened in 1873 and soon turned into a meeting place for Austro-Hungarian nobility. It still retains its regal charm. Delights from the hotel's con- fectioners include the Imperialtorte, created to honour Emperor Franz Joseph I at the hotel's opening.

Marriott Vienna
MAP P5 ■ Parkring 12a ■ 01 515 180 ■ www. viennamarriott.at ■ €€€
The Marriott is within walking distance of all the famous landmarks. It has an indoor swimming pool and a health club where guests can relax after a hard day's sightseeing.

Palais Coburg Hotel Residenz
MAP P4 ■ Coburgbastei 4 ■ 01 518 180 ■ www. palais-coburg.com ■ €€€
This luxurious hotel is housed in a 19th-century building. There are health and beauty facilities, and the Coburg spa on the top floor offers good views.

Radisson Blu Palais Hotel Vienna
MAP P5 ■ Parkring 16 ■ 01 515 170 ■ www. radissonblu.com/ palaishotel-vienna ■ €€€
The Palais Leitenberger and the Palais Henckel von Donnersmarck were

converted into this five-star hotel in the late 20th century. The hotel has non-smoking and anti-allergy rooms.

Vienna Intercontinental

MAP Q6 ▪ Johannes-gasse 28 ▪ 01 711 220 ▪ www.intercontinental.com/Vienna ▪ €€€
This luxurious five-star modern hotel occupies a convenient location opposite the Stadtpark and not far from the Konzerthaus. It offers 453 plush rooms that guarantee a pleasant stay.

Hotels in Great Locations

Seminarhotel Springer Schlössl

Tivoligasse 73 ▪ Bus 9A ▪ 01 814 20 49 ▪ www.springer-schloessl.at ▪ €
Housed in a castle built in 1887 and set in a large park near the famous Schloss Schönbrunn, this hotel has good facilities for business travellers.

Das Opernring

MAP M5 ▪ Opernring 11 ▪ 01 587 55 18 ▪ www.opernring.at ▪ €€
This hotel in the grand Historicist style of the Ringstrasse is opposite the Staatsoper. The balconies overlook the tree-lined Ring and offer great views along the boulevard. No air-conditioning.

Hotel Park-Villa

Hasenauerstrasse 12 ▪ Bus 40A ▪ 01 367 57 00 ▪ www.parkvilla.at ▪ €€
Situated in the elegant Döbling neighbourhood, this magnificent villa turned hotel was once used by well-off Viennese to spend their summers. Most rooms have balconies and the terrace leads into the garden.

Hotel Regina

MAP C3 ▪ Rooseveltplatz 15 ▪ 01 404 460 ▪ www.kremslehnerhotels.at ▪ €€
The Hotel Regina has a terrific view of the Neo-Gothic Votivkirche, with rooms overlooking the church's roof and its high stone towers. Besides the popular hotel café, the stylish Roth restaurant can be found on the ground floor. There is no air-conditioning.

Hotel Schloss Wilhelminenberg

Savoyenstrasse 2 ▪ Bus 146B ▪ 01 485 85 03 ▪ www.austria-trend.at ▪ €€
Count Lascy, an Austrian aristocrat, had this palace built between 1781 and 1784 on his hunting grounds on top of the Wilhelminen mountain. The hotel offers great views of Vienna and is very well located – it only takes about 30 minutes to get here from the city centre. The hotel has no air-conditioning.

Grand Hotel Wien

MAP N6 ▪ Kärntner Ring 9 ▪ 01 515 800 ▪ www.grandhotelwien.com ▪ €€€
Opened in 1870, the Grand Hotel Wien is housed in an elegant mansion located along the Ringstrasse and has an early 20th-century feel. It has 250 luxurious rooms and suites, which are decorated in Art Nouveau style.

Hilton Vienna Danube Waterfront

Handelskai 269 ▪ Train Handelskai; U-Bahn U6 ▪ 01 72 777 ▪ www3.hilton.com ▪ €€€
Close to the football stadium, this luxury accommodation has an outdoor pool on the riverbank, and advertises itself as "Austria's leading business hotel".

Hotel Am Stephansplatz

MAP N3 ▪ Stephansplatz 9 ▪ 01 534 050 ▪ www.hotelamstephansplatz.at ▪ €€€
Situated in the heart of Vienna, this hotel has first-class amenities. Many rooms have a view of the cathedral.

The Ring

MAP N6 ▪ Kärntner Ring 8 ▪ 01 22 122 ▪ www.theringhotel.com ▪ €€€
Located directly on the Ring, just a stone's throw away from the Staatsoper and main shopping district, the rooms at this boutique hotel are sumptuously decorated in a contemporary style. There is a well-equipped fitness room, steam bath, sauna or full-service spa.

Sans Souci

MAP E1 ▪ Burggasse 2 ▪ 01 522 25 20 ▪ www.sanssouci-wien.com ▪ €€€
Steps away from the MuseumsQuartier, this place is right in the centre of Vienna's hippest area. Facilities include a swimming pool and spa, and all rooms are air-conditioned and individually designed. It is a remarkable blend of traditional architecture and contemporary comfort.

Historic Hotels

Hotel Orient
MAP M2 ■ Tiefer Graben
30–32 ■ 01 533 72 07
■ www.hotelorient.at ■ €
Established in 1896, the
Hotel Orient is on an old
riverbank that linked the
city with the Danube. It
was here that trading
ships unloaded cargo
from the Orient years
ago. The hotel is fitted
with an opulent *fin-de-
siècle* interior, but note
that many of the rooms
are rented by the hour.
No air-conditioning.

Pertschy Palais Hotel
MAP M3 ■
Habsburgergasse
5 ■ 01 534 490 ■ www.
pertschy.com ■ €
Aristocrat Maximilian von
Cavriani had a Baroque
palace built here in 1734.
The lovely building is now
a privately run B&B with
an inner courtyard and
55 rooms fitted with
modern amenities.

Ambassador
MAP N4 ■ Neuer Markt
5/Kärntner Strasse 22 ■
01 961 610 ■ www.
ambassador.at ■ €€
Baroque architect Fischer
von Erlach constructed
this house in the late 17th
century and in 1898 it
became a hotel. Famous
guests have included the
writer Mark Twain and
actress Marlene Dietrich.
It's still one of Vienna's
most charming hotels.

Hotel König von Ungarn
MAP N3 ■ Schulerstrasse
10 ■ 01 515 840 ■ www.
kvu.at ■ €€
As early as 1815 the "King
of Hungary" hotel was
established in this historic
building that dates back
to the 1600s. During the
Austro-Hungarian
monarchy, Hungarian
aristocrats used to rent
apartments here all year
round. Many of their
names are inscribed in
the hotel's guest book.

Hotel Mailbergerhof
MAP N5 ■ Annagasse 7
■ 01 512 06 41 ■ www.
mailbergerhof.at ■ €€
The history of this
fascinating house dates
back to the 14th century,
although the original
Gothic building was
converted into a small
Baroque palace with
stables and its own
chapel. The 40 well-
appointed non-smoking
rooms are cosy.

Hotel Rathauspark
MAP J2 ■ Rathausstrasse
17 ■ 01 404 120 ■ www.
austria-trend.at ■ €€
This hotel was the home
of the Austrian writer
Stefan Zweig and you
can still experience the
atmosphere of imperial
Vienna here. It is close
to the Town Hall and the
iconic Café Central. No
air-conditioning.

Mercure Grand Hotel Biedermeier Wien
MAP R4 ■ Landstrasser
Hauptstrasse 28 ■ 01 716
710 ■ www.accorhotels.
com ■ €€
Housed in an early
19th-century building in
a peaceful location, this
hotel is within walking
distance of Stephansdom,
the Belvedere and the
Ring. The charming
Biedermeier house has a
quiet inner courtyard and
a conservatory restaurant.
Pets are allowed for
an additional €10.

Parkhotel Schönbrunn
Hietzinger Hauptstrasse
10–20 ■ Tram 58 ■ 01 878
040 ■ www.austria-
trend.at ■ €€
Emperor Franz Joseph I
had this stately mansion
built in 1907 in the Hietzing
district near Schloss
Schönbrunn to accom-
modate his guests. The
hotel offers modern ame-
nities and has more than
a hint of the imperial
splendour of bygone days.
No air-conditioning.

Römischer Kaiser
MAP N5 ■ Annagasse 16
■ 01 512 77 510 ■ www.
hotel-roemischer-kaiser.
at ■ €€
This hotel is housed in a
Baroque palace dating
from 1684 in a side street
off Kärntner Strasse. The
foyer and some rooms
still have historic features.

Wandl
MAP M3 ■ Petersplatz
9 ■ 01 534 550 ■ www.
hotel-wandl.com ■ €€
This family-run hotel is in a
house that dates back to
1700. It has friendly guest
rooms and a large foyer
but no air-conditioning.

Family-Friendly Hotels

Art Hotel
Brandmayergasse 9 ■ 01
544 51 08 ■ www.theart
hotelvienna.at ■ €
There is a lot of art, as
the name suggests, but
also inexpensive large
family rooms with kitch-
ens, and underground
parking. Located near the
colourful street market
Naschmarkt, the hotel
is just 20 minutes away by
bus from Stephansdom.
No air-conditioning.

Hotel Anatol
MAP G1 ■ Webgasse 26
■ 01 599 960 ■ www.
austria-trend.at/hotel-
anatol ■ €
Around the corner from
Mariahilfer Strasse, Hotel
Anatol has large family
rooms, but all without
air-conditioning. Toys are
available and a babysitter
can be arranged.

Das Capri
MAP R1 ■ Praterstrasse
44–6 ■ 01 214 84 04
■ www.dascapri.at
■ €€
Centrally situated halfway
between Stephansdom
and the Prater amuse-
ment park, this family-
run hotel offers modern
family rooms and spacious
suites, but there is no air-
conditioning. Every room
comes with free use of a
Samsung tablet.

Erzherzog Rainer
MAP G4 ■ Wiedner
Hauptstrasse 27–29
■ 01 221 11 ■ www.
schick-hotels.com ■ €€
A short walk from the
Belvedere Palace, this
large, old-fashioned hotel
is one of the five Vienna
Schick family hotels.
Children are warmly
welcomed and babysitting
is available. All rooms are
non-smoking, but there
is no air-conditioning.

The Harmonie
MAP B3 ■ Harmoniegasse
5–7 ■ 01 317 66 04
■ www.harmonie-vienna.
at ■ €€
Stylish and comfortable
boutique hotel, serving
free tea and cakes in
the lounge and library.
Rooms are decorated
with paintings by artist
Luis Casanova Sorolla,
making them unique.

Hotel am Parkring
MAP Q4 ■ Parkring
12 ■ 01 514 800 ■ www.
schick-hotels.com ■ €€
Located on the elegant
Ringstrasse, the 58-room
Hotel am Parkring offers
a splendid view of the
tree-lined avenue from
the 13th floor. It is a great
choice for families. For
its younger guests, plenty
of books and toys are
available and babysitters
can be easily organized.
The restaurant also offers
children's menus.

Hotel City Central
MAP Q1 ■ Taborstrasse
8 ■ 01 211 050 ■ www.
schick-hotels.com ■ €€
Located on the edge of
the city centre, this is an
ideal point from which to
discover the city. This
four-star hotel was built
at the beginning of the
20th century. Children
under six stay free; those
between six and twelve
stay for half price.

Hotel Lassalle
Engerthstrasse 173–5
■ U-Bahn U1 ■ 01 213
150 ■ www.austria-
trend.at ■ €€
This modern hotel is
ideally situated for families, as the Danube island
with all its lawns and
cycling paths is close by.
There are family rooms,
a games room and play-
room for children with
toys and books. You can
arrange babysitters on
request at reception. No
air-conditioning.

Hotel Stefanie
MAP Q1 ■ Taborstrasse
12 ■ 01 211 500 ■ www.
schick-hotels.com ■ €€
Named after the wife of
Crown Prince Rudolph,
Hotel Stefanie is located

just beyond the Danube
canal and only a few
minutes' walk from the
city centre. Toys and
special children's menus
are available, as well as
reliable babysitting ser-
vices. Of the hotel's 131
guest rooms, some are
extra-large accommoda-
tion meant for families.

Mercure Josefshof Wien
MAP D2 ■ Josefsgasse
4–6 ■ 01 404 190 ■ www.
josefshof.com ■ €€
This hotel is found on a
quiet road in a central
location. Breakfast is
served until noon. The
Mercure is a good choice
for families as one child
under the age of 16 can
stay for free in a room
with two parents.

Starlight Suite Hotel Wien am Heumarkt
MAP E6 ■ Am Heumarkt
15 ■ 01 710 78 08 ■ www.
starlighthotels.com ■ €€
Next to the Stadtpark, this
modern hotel offers large
suites, as well as regular
bedrooms. Free break-
fast is available. Children
under the age of 12 stay
free of charge.

Medium-Priced Hotels

Am Schottenpoint
MAP B3 ■ Währinger
Strasse 22 ■ 01 310 87 87
■ www.schottenpoint.at
■ €
This small hotel is a
friendly place with 17
non-air-conditioned
rooms. It's within walking
distance of the Ring and
only a few minutes from
the tram, bus and under-
ground services into the
centre. A breakfast buffet
is included.

Carlton Opera

MAP F3 ▪ Schikaneder-gasse 4 ▪ 01 587 53 02 ▪ www.carlton.at ▪ €
Located on the edge of the city centre, the Carlton Opera is an ideal starting point for exploring the city. Karlskirche is just around the corner and the MuseumsQuartier is also nearby. All its 57 rooms have tea- and coffee-making facilities. Apartments with family rooms and a kitchen are also available.

Congress

MAP H5 ▪ Wiedner Gürtel 34 ▪ 01 505 55 06 ▪ www.novum-hotels.de ▪ €
This modern three-star hotel is set very close to the Belvedere. Situated just across from the former Südbahnhof on a fairly busy road, it offers good value. All 75 rooms and two apartments are non-air-conditioned and have satellite television as well as internet access.

Cryston

MAP H1 ▪ Gaudenzdorfer Gürtel 63 ▪ 01 813 56 82 ▪ www.hotel-cryston.at ▪ €
The cosy, friendly rooms of the Hotel Cryston make up for its location on a busy road. The modern bedrooms are fitted with satellite TV, direct-dial phones, a safe, and hairdryers in the en-suite bathrooms, but there is no air-conditioning.

Daniel Wien

MAP H6 ▪ Landstrasser Gürtel 5 ▪ 01 901 310 ▪ www.hoteldaniel.com/vienna ▪ €
This smart, minimalist hotel in the Belvedere quarter has its own bakery on site. Guests can hire iPads and Vespa scooters. You can even sleep in a luxury 1952 aluminium Airstream trailer in the garden.

Marc Aurel

MAP N2 ▪ Marc-Aurel-Strasse 8 ▪ 01 533 36 40 ▪ www.hotel-marcaurel.com ▪ €
Within walking distance of Stephansdom, this hotel has 18 rooms, some of them suitable for people with specific needs. There are also two large rooms with a kitchenette.

Ruby Marie

Kaiserstrasse 2–4 ▪ 01 361 966 066 ▪ www.ruby-hotels.com ▪ €
Near the Westbahnhof, the Ruby Marie hotel is trendy but offers amazing value for money. The rooftop bar area is large, and has great views. Both bikes and electric guitars are available for hire here and there is also a yoga space and a library, as well as a 25-seat cinema for guests.

Alma Boutique-Hotel

MAP P2 ▪ Hafnersteig 7 ▪ 01 533 29 61 ▪ www.hotel-alma.com ▪ €€
The once modest Pension Christina has undergone a complete makeover and now boasts stylish decor in shades of gold, red and brown. The hotel's 26 rooms are fitted out with a range of amenities, including whirlpool baths in some rooms. Located in the heart of Vienna, it is within walking distance of the famous sights. Visitors can also enjoy excellent views of the city from the terrace.

Hotel Austria

MAP P2 ▪ Fleischmarkt 20 ▪ 01 515 23 ▪ www.hotelaustria-wien.at ▪ €€
The Hotel Austria, located in a cul-de-sac, offers peace and quiet even though it is in the middle of Vienna. It has 42 rooms and four apartments, and there is also the cheaper option of picking a room without an en-suite. No air-conditioning.

Hotel Prinz Eugen

MAP H5 ▪ Wiedner Gürtel 14 ▪ 01 505 17 41 ▪ www.novum-hotels.com/hotel-prinz-eugen-wien ▪ €€
This standard city hotel is situated in the embassy district, close to the Belvedere. The decor is an eclectic mix – some of the rooms are traditional and some are modern.

Rathaus Wine & Design

MAP D2 ▪ Lange Gasse 13 ▪ 01 400 11 22 ▪ Closed 22–27 Dec ▪ www.hotel-rathaus-wien.at ▪ €€
In this designer hotel close to the city centre everything revolves around wine. Each of the rooms is dedicated to a top Austrian wine-grower, there is a wine and cheese breakfast, and there are wine cosmetics in the rooms.

Budget Hotels

Ani

Kinderspitalgasse 1 ▪ U-Bahn U6 ▪ 01 405 65 53 ▪ www.freerooms.at ▪ €
Pension Ani is a simple B&B in an old building with rooms in various sizes, but there is no air-conditioning. It is located close to the underground U6 and trams.

Boltzmann

MAP B2 ■ Boltzmann-gasse 8 ■ 01 354 500 ■ www.hotelboltzmann.at ■ €
This hotel, set near the Gartenpalais Liechtenstein in the Alsergrund quarter, is in an ideal location for exploring Vienna on foot. It is child-friendly and smokers are relegated to two floors. The attractive courtyard garden, underground parking and reasonable room rates mean that early booking is strongly advised.

Drei Kronen Wien City

MAP F4 ■ Schleifmühlgasse 25 ■ 01 587 32 89 ■ www.hotel3kronen.at ■ €
Although the building is more than 100 years old, the Drei Kronen Wien City hotel has modern, individually furnished rooms, all equipped with a TV and internet access. However, there's no air-conditioning. Located in one of the city's booming areas, near the Secession Building and Karlskirche, with many restaurants, pubs and bars nearby. There's also a good breakfast buffet.

Haydn

MAP F2 ■ Mariahilfer Strasse 57–9 ■ 01 587 44 140 ■ www.haydn-hotel.at ■ €
This three-star hotel is set on one of Vienna's main shopping streets, Mariahilfer Strasse, and has an underground station right by its front door. The rooms are quiet and are equipped with a telephone, cable TV and a minibar. The hotel also has other options such as apartments with kitchen facilities and suites.

Hotel Bleckmann

MAP C3 ■ Währinger Strasse 15 ■ 01 408 08 99 ■ www.hotelbleckmann.at ■ €
This cosy family-run hotel is set in the Schottenring and Alsergrund quarter, where Sigmund Freud, Franz Schubert and many other famous Viennese personalities lived. The rooms are simple and nicely furnished, though not air-conditioned, and there is a breakfast buffet.

Kaffeemühle

Kaiserstrasse 45 ■ 01 523 86 88 ■ www.novum-hotels.com/hotel-kaffeemuehle-wien ■ €
Acquired by the Novum hotel chain, the "Coffee Mill" offers stylish urban design with no frills attached. Its location in the hip Neubau area of the city enables convenient access to public transport. Clean and remarkably inexpensive, the rooms are unsurprisingly in very high demand, so early booking is advised. Guests should note that there is no air-conditioning.

Kolping Gästehaus

MAP F3 ■ Stiegengasse 12/Ecke Gumpendorfer Strasse ■ 01 587 56 310 ■ www.kolping-wien-zentral.at ■ €
Located in a small side street not far from the MuseumsQuartier, most of the modern rooms in this guest house are very quiet. There's a wide range of non-air-conditioned rooms to suit all budgets, and visitors can choose between various sizes and standards of accommodation. A breakfast buffet is also available.

Kugel

MAP E2 ■ Siebensterngasse 43 ■ 01 523 33 55 ■ Closed 9 Jan–29 Feb ■ www.hotelkugel.at ■ €
Hotel Kugel, located next to the Spittelberg area, has been in operation since 1899. It offers free Wi-Fi, a relaxed atmosphere and tasteful rooms, some with four-poster beds. There is no air-conditioning.

Nossek

MAP M3 ■ Graben 17 ■ 01 533 70 41 11 ■ No credit cards ■ www.pension-nossek.at ■ €
This B&B is located in the pedestrian zone of Graben, right in the middle of the bustling city centre. Its 26 rooms are cosy and fitted with all mod cons. There is also a TV room, and families are welcome.

Vienna Westend City Hostel

Fügergasse 3 ■ U-Bahn U3, U6 ■ 01 597 67 290 ■ No credit cards ■ www.viennahostel.at ■ €
This hostel close to the Westbahnhof railway station has simple non-air-conditioned rooms at good rates. The building has a spiral staircase but there is also a lift and a small garden. Facilities include a bike-locker room and a communal TV room. Rooms are available at a broad range of rates.

Zur Wiener Staatsoper

MAP N5 ■ Krugerstrasse 11 ■ 01 513 12 74 ■ www.zurwienerstaatsoper.at ■ €
Non-air-conditioned rooms of various sizes and a breakfast buffet are offered at this family-run hotel in a top location in the heart of Vienna.

For a key to hotel price categories see p142

Index

Acknowledgments

Author
British-born journalist and broadcaster Michael Leidig has been the *Daily Telegraph* and *Sunday Telegraph* Vienna correspondent since 1995, as well as the editor of the English-language newspaper the *Vienna Reporter* and presenter of the Austrian Broadcasting Corporation's English News service. He has lived in Austria since 1993.

Austrian journalist and broadcaster Irene Zoech has been *The Times* correspondent in Vienna since 1999, as well as Arts and Culture Editor for the English-language newspaper *Austria Today* since 1995. She is also News Editor at the press agency Central European News.

Additional contributor
Sarah Woods

Publishing Director Georgina Dee

Publisher Vivien Antwi

Design Director Phil Ormerod

Editorial Sophie Adam, Ankita Awasthi Tröger, Michelle Crane, Rebecca Flynn, Rachel Fox, Becky Miles, Sally Schafer, Beverly Smart, Hollie Teague

Cover Design: Richard Czapnik

Design Marisa Renzullo, Stuti Tiwari, Priyanka Thakur, Vinita Venugopal

Picture Research Susie Peachey, Ellen Root, Lucy Sienkowska

Cartography Suresh Kumar, James Macdonald, Casper Morris, Animesh Pathak

DTP Jason Little

Production Igrain Roberts

Factchecker Doug Sager

Proofreader Kathryn Glendenning

Indexer Helen Peters

Illustrator Chris Orr & Associates
chrisorr.com

First edition created by Sargasso Media Ltd, London

Commissioned Photography Clive Streeter, Peter Wilson

Picture Credits
The publisher would like to thank the following for their kind permission to reproduce their photographs:
Key: a-above; b-below/bottom; c-centre; f-far; l-left; r-right; t-top

123RF.com: Andrey Andronov 92bc, ginasanders 106cla, Kabvisio 74tr, kisamarkiza 91t, Pavel Lipskiy 83b, 102b, Meinzahn 122b, Alexandr Mychko 75bl, Roman Plesky 100ca, Anna Pustynnikova 75tr, radub85 107b, 117cla, tasfoto 81br, Yaroslav Yatsyk 126cla, zechal 116ca.

Alamy Stock Photo: blickwinkel / Samot 105cl; Ian Dagnall 34–5; DanitaDelimont.com / Rob Tilley 1; Svetlana Dingarac 87tr; edpics 67cl, 72bl; EU / Peter Forsberg 108tc; Manfred Gottschalk 40clb; Granger Historical Picture Archive 48ca; Hackenberg-Photo-Cologne 80tl, 80br, 99tr, 116b; Hemis.fr / Ludovic Maisant 29tl;

imageBROKER / Egon Bömsch 32cla; John Kellerman 26–7; Brian_Kinney 10cla; Art Kowalsky 2tl, 3tr, 8–9, 66b, 132–3; LOOK Die Bildagentur der Fotografen GmbH / Ingolf Pompe 50tr; Stefano Politi Markovina 4cl; McPhoto / Bilderbox 14cl; David Noton 10clb; Prisma by Dukas Presseagentur GmbH 43ca; Romas_ph 3tl, 88–9; Sagaphoto.com / Stephane Gautier 73tr; Riccardo Sala 29cr; Maurice Savage 18cra; travelimages 4cra; Lucas Vallecillos 16–7; Ernst Wrba 45br; Zoonar / David Ryan 81cla.

© Albertina, Vienna: 7cla, 91crb.

AWL Images: Jon Arnold 112–3; Neil Farrin 10bl; Stefano Politi Markovina 11clb.

B&F Wien: Manfred Seidl 67tl.

Belvedere, Vienna: 28bl, 28–9, 31bl.

Bildarchiv Österreichische Nationalbibliothek, Wien: 19tr; Johannes Hloch 18bl.

Burgtheater: 93cl.

Café Do-An: 119cla.

Café Museum: 118ca.

Circus and Clown Museum: 57tr.

Das Mo öbel: 110b.

Das Triest: 125b.

© Palais Daun-Kinsky, Wien: Herbert Lehmann 51cl.

Der Dritte Mann Tour: Felicitas Matern 64tl.

Dorotheum: R. R. Rumpler 97tl.

Dreamstime.com: Abxyz 4crb; Alexirina27000 17tl; David Bailey 52cl, 62tr; Maksim Budnikov 101bc; Nikolay Bychkov 36br; Chaoss 6bl, 73cl; Dafrei 50tl; Dagobert1620 130b; Digitalpress 55bl; Mindauga Dulinska 12cl, 41tl; Dziewul 40cr, 128tr; Darius Dzinnin 75cl; Empire331 85cl; Denitsa Glavinova 44cl; Özgür Güvenç 53t; Fritz Hiersche 129cla; Kisamarkiza 44b, 86tl; Derii Larisa 74bl; Pavel Lipskiy 38br, 59b; Anna Lurye 54t; Marcin Łukaszewicz 11tl; Magition 32br; Meinzahn 4t, 65tr, 70–1, 104b; Mikolaj64 84tl; minnystock 17cr; Mircea Hotea 78tr; Ncristian 11br; Olgalngs 15crb; Lefteris Papaulakis 12–3; Pavel068 11cla; Bojan Pavlukovic 90cla; Photoblueice 51br; Radub85 56br, 58clb; Romasph 7tr, 115br; Rosshelen 64b; Jozef Sedmak 101t, 120cla; Sjankauskas 60bc; Nikolai Sorokin 18tl; Calin-andrei Stan 87cla; Svetlana195 4b, 52bc, 61br; TasFoto 16cla, 41crb, 85tr, 102tl; Tomas1111 36cl, 92cl, 94bl; Varandah 10crb; Vitalyedush 12clb; Voltan1 63tr; Bettina Wagner 4cla; Xalanx 13tr; Alex Zarubin 4clb; Minyun Zhou 33br.

Fabios: 99clb.

Getty Images: adoc-photos 19bl; AFP / Patrick Domingo 6tr, / Joe Klamar 83tr, / Dieter Nagl 84b; Gonzalo Azumendi 115tl; De Agostini Picture Library 60clb; DEA / A. Dagli Orti 45clb, 49tr, 61cl, / E. Lessing 31tr, / G. Dagli Orti 60tr; Pascal Deloche 2tr, 46–7, 127t; Godong 79cla; Jorg Greuel 121b; Hulton Deutsch 49cl; Hulton Fine Art Collection 48b; Imagno 15cla, 21b, 30tr, 37tl, 92tr; Herbert Neubauer 72t; Sylvain Sonnet 33tl; UIG / JTB Photo 121tr; Ullstein Bild 15clb, / Karin Nussbaumer 70crb.

Haus der Musik: Rudi Froese 57cl.

ImPulsTanz: Karolina Miernik 86cr.

iStockphoto.com: alessandro0770 37bl.

© **KHM-Museumsverband:** 22cra, 22cl, 22bl, 23tl, 23cra, 24cl, 24bl, 25tr, 25c, 25b.

Kunsthalle: Installation view: Political Populism, Kunsthalle Wien 2015, Photo: Stephan Wyckoff: Goshka Macuga, Model for a Sculpture (Family), 2011, Courtesy the artist and Andrew Kreps Gallery, New York; Of what is, that it is; Of what is not, that it is not 1, 2012, Courtesy the artist and Prada Collection, Mailand 59tl.

Leopold Museum, Vienna: Self, Portrait with Chinese Lantern Plant (1912) Egon Schiele, Oil, opaque color on wood, 32,2 × 39,8 cm 11cra; WienTourismus / Peter Rigaud 35tl.

Marionettentheater Schloss Schönbrunn: Roman Gerhardt 68t.

Meinl am Graben: Herbert Lehmann 96bc; Ludwig Schedl 77crb.

Meixner's Gastwirtschaft: 131cra.

MuseumsQuartier E+B GesmbH: Hertha Hurnaus 108-9.

Österreichische Akademie der Wissenschaften: Klaus Pichler 94tr.

© **Palais Ferstel, Vienna:** Christian Husar 78-9; Herbert Lehmann 98b; Michael Rzepa 50br.

Salm Bräu: Mario Kranabetter 124tl.

Copyright Schloss Schönbrunn Kultur- und Betriebsges.m.b.H.: 42bl, 43bl; Bildagentur Zolles KG / Christian Hofer 42c; Knaack 17br; Lois Lammerhuber 128-9; Julius Silver 62b.

Sigmund Freud Museum: Oliver Ottenschlaeger 103cla.

Sky Bar: 95b.

Spanish Riding School: ASAblanca.com / Rene é van Bakel 20t, 20c; Mathias Lauringer 20bl.

Steffl: Michael Sazel 82t.

Steirereck im Stadtpark: © pierer.net 76b.

SuperStock: 14br, 86-7; age fotostock / Carlos S. Pereyra 41bl; F1 ONLINE 55cra; imageBROKER 79tr.

Tanzquartier Wien GmbH: Boom Bodies / Christine Sbaschnigg 35cla.

Technisches Museum Wien: 68clb; Peter Sedlaczek 56t.

Tunnel: 111cla.

Vienna Secession: Jorit Aust 39tl; Oliver Ottenschlaeger 38-9; Wolfgang Thaler 11cr, 39br.

© **www.lupispuma.com / Volkstheater:** 70tl, 107tl.

Wein & Co Bar: 118br.

WEINZIRL Restaurant im Konzerthaus: 77tl.

Wien Museum: Hertha Hurnaus 123tl, 127br.

Xocolat: 96cl.

Zoom Kindermuseum: Alexandra Eizinger 69cra; J. J. Kucek 34bl.

Cover
Front and spine: **500px:** Christian Thür.
Back: **Dreamstime.com:** Sorin Colac.

Pull Out Map Cover
500px: Christian Thür.

All other images © Dorling Kindersley
For furt'her information see:
www.dkimages.com

As a guide to abbreviations in visitor information blocks: **Adm** = *admission charge;* **DA** = *disabled access;* **D** = *dinner;* **L** = *lunch.*

Penguin
Random
House

Printed and bound in China

First published in Great Britain in 2003 by Dorling Kindersley Limited 80 Strand, London WC2R 0RL

Copyright 2003, 2018 © Dorling Kindersley Limited

A Penguin Random House Company

18 19 20 21 10 9 8 7 6 5 4 3 2 1

Reprinted with revisions 2005, 2007, 2009, 2011, 2013, 2015, 2018

MIX
Paper from
responsible sources
FSC
www.fsc.org   FSC™ C018179

SPECIAL EDITIONS OF DK TRAVEL GUIDES

DK Travel Guides can be purchased in bulk quantities at discounted prices for use in promotions or as premiums. We are also able to offer special editions and personalized jackets, corporate imprints, and excerpts from all of our books, tailored specifically to meet your own needs.

To find out more, please contact:

in the US
specialsales@dk.com

in the UK
travelguides@uk.dk.com

in Canada
specialmarkets@dk.com

in Australia
penguincorporatesales@penguinrandomhouse.com.au

Phrase Book

In an Emergency

Where is the telephone?	Wo ist das Telefon?	voh ist duss tel-e-fone?
Help!	Hilfe!	hilf-uh
Please call a doctor	Bitte rufen Sie einen Arzt	bitt-uh roof'n zee ine-en artst
Please call the police	Bitte rufen Sie die Polizei	bitt-uh roof'n zee dee poli-tsy
Please call the fire brigade	Bitte rufen Sie die Feuerwehr	bitt-uh roof'n zee dee foyer-vayr
Stop!	Halt!	hult

Communication Essentials

Yes	Ja	yah
No	Nein	nine
Please	Bitte	bitt-uh
Thank you	Danke	dunk-uh
Excuse me	Verzeihung	fair-tsy-hoong
Hello (good day)	Guten Tag	goot-en tahk
Goodbye	Auf Wiedersehen	owf-veed-er-zay-ern
Good evening	Guten Abend	goot'n ahb'nt
Good night	Gute Nacht	goot-uh nukht
Why?	Warum?	var-room
Where?	Wo?	voh
When?	Wann?	vunn
today	heute	hoyt-uh
tomorrow	morgen	morg'n
month	Monat	mohn-aht
night	Nacht	nukht
afternoon	Nachmittag	nahkh-mit-tahk
morning	Morgen	morg'n
year	Jahr	yar
there	dort	dort
here	hier	hear
week	Woche	vokh-uh
yesterday	gestern	gest'n
evening	Abend	ahb'nt

Useful Phrases

How are you?	Wie geht's?	vee gayts
Fine, thanks	Danke, es geht mir gut	dunk-uh, es gayt meer goot
Where is/are?	Wo ist/sind...?	voh ist/sind
How far is it to...?	Wie weit ist es...?	vee vite ist ess
Do you speak English?	Sprechen Sie Englisch?	shpresh'n zee eng-glish
I don't understand	Ich verstehe nicht	ish fair-shtay-uh nisht
Please speak more slowly	Bitte, sprechen Sie langsamer	bitte shpresh'n zee lang-zammer

Useful Words

large	gross	grohss
small	klein	kline
hot	heiss	hyce
cold	kalt	kult
good	gut	goot
bad	böse/schlecht	burss-uh/shlesht
open	geöffnet	g'urff-nett
closed	geschlossen	g'shloss'n
left	links	links
right	rechts	reshts

Making a Telephone Call

I would like to make a phone call	Ich möchte telefonieren	ish mer-shtuh tel-e-fon-eer'n
I'll try again later	Ich versuche noch ein mal später	ish fair-zookh-uh r nokh ine-mull shpay-te
Can I leave a message?	Kann ich eine Nachricht hinterlassen?	kan ish ine-uh nakh-risht hint-er-lahss-en
telephone card	Telefonkarte	tel-e-fohn-kart-uh
mobile phone	Mobiltelefon	mobeel tel-e-fone
engaged (busy)	besetzt	b'zetst
wrong number	Falsche Verbindung	falsh-uh fair-bin-doong

Sightseeing

entrance ticket	Eintrittskarte	ine-tritz-kart-uh
cemetery	Friedhof	freed-hofe
train station	Bahnhof	barn-hofe
gallery	Galerie	gall-er-ree
information	Auskunft	owss-koonft
church	Kirche	keersh-uh
garden	Garten	gart'n
palace/castle	Palast/Schloss	pallast/shloss
place (square)	Platz	plats
bus stop	Haltestelle	hal-te-shtel-uh
national holiday	Nationalfeiertag	nats-yon-ahl-fire-tahk
theatre	Theater	tay-aht-er
free admission	Eintritt frei	ine-tritt fry

Shopping

Do you have...?	Gibt es...?	geept ess
How much does it cost?	Was kostet das?	voss kost't duss?
When do you open/close?	Wann öffnen Sie? schliessen Sie?	vunn off'n zee shlees'n zee
this	das	duss
expensive	teuer	toy-er
cheap	preiswert	price-vurt
size	Grösse	gruhs-uh
number	Nummer	noom-er
colour	Farbe	farb-uh
brown	braun	brown
black	schwarz	shvarts
red	rot	roht
blue	blau	blau
green	grün	groon
yellow	gelb	gelp

Types of Shop

antiques shop	Antiquariat	antik-var-yat
chemist (pharmacy)	Apotheke/ Drogerie	appo-tay-kuh/ droog-er-ree
bank	Bank	bunk
market	Markt	markt
travel agency	Reisebüro	rye-zer-boo-roe
department store	Warenhaus	vahr'n-hows
hairdresser	Friseur	freezz-er
newspaper kiosk	Zeitungskiosk	tsytoongs-kee-osk
bookshop	Buchhandlung	bookh-hant-loong
bakery	Bäckerei	beck-er-eye
post office	Post	posst
shop/store	Geschäft/Laden	gush-eft/lard'n
shoe shop	Schuhladen	shoo-lard'n
clothes shop	Kleiderladen, Boutique	klyder-lard'n boo-teek-uh
food shop	Lebensmittel- geschäft	lay-bens-mittel-gush-eft

Staying in a Hotel

Do you have any vacancies?	Haben Sie noch Zimmer frei?	harb'n zee nokh tsimm-er-fry
with twin beds?	mit zwei Betten?	mitt tsvy bett'n
with a double bed?	mit einem Doppelbett?	mitt ine'm dopp'l-bet
with a bath?	mit Bad?	mitt bart
with a shower?	mit Dusche?	mitt doosh-uh
I have a reservation	Ich habe eine Reservierung	ish harb-uh ine-uh rez-er-veer-oong
key	Schlüssel	shlooss'l
porter	Pförtner	pfert-ner

Eating Out

Do you have a table for…?	Haben Sie einen Tisch für…?	harb'n zee ine-uhn tish foor
I would like to reserve a table	Ich möchte eine Reservierung machen	ish mer-shtuh ine-uh rezer-veer-oong-makh'n
Waiter!	Herr Ober!	hair oh-bare!
The bill (check)	Die Rechnung	dee resh-noong
breakfast	Frühstück	froo-shtook
lunch	Mittagessen	mit-targ-ess'n
dinner	Abendessen	arb'nt-ess'n
bottle	Flasche	flush-uh
dish of the day	Tagesgericht	tahg-es-gur-isht
main dish	Hauptgericht	howpt-gur-isht
dessert	Nachtisch	nahkh-tish
cup	Tasse	tass-uh
wine list	Weinkarte	vine-kart-uh
glass	Glas	glars
spoon	Löffel	lerff'l
tip	Trinkgeld	trink-gelt
knife	Messer	mess-er
starter (appetizer)	Vorspeise	for-shpize-uh
plate	Teller	tell-er
fork	Gabel	gahb'l

Menu Decoder

Beefsteack	beef-stayk	steak
Bier	beer	beer
Branntwein	brant-vine	spirits
Bratkartoffeln	brat-kar-toff'ln	fried potatoes
Bratwurst	brat-voorst	fried sausage
Brötchen	bret-tchen	bread roll
Brot	brot	bread
Brühe	bruh-uh	broth
Butter	boot-ter	butter
Champignon	shum-pin-yong	mushroom
Ei	eye	egg
Eis	ice	ice/ice cream
Ente	ent-uh	duck
Fisch	fish	fish
Forelle	for-ell-uh	trout
Frikadelle	Frika-dayl-uh	hamburger
Gans	ganns	goose
Garnele	gar-nayl-uh	prawn/shrimp
gebraten	g'braat'n	fried
gegrillt	g'grilt	grilled
gekocht	g'kokht	boiled
geräuchert	g'rowk-ert	smoked
Gemüse	g'mooz-uh	vegetables
Hähnchen	haynsh'n	chicken
Kaffee	kaf-fay	coffee
Kalbfleisch	kalp-flysh	veal
Karpfen	karpf'n	carp
Käse	kayz-uh	cheese
Knoblauch	k'nob-lowkh	garlic
Knödel	k'nerd'l	noodle
Kohl	koal	cabbage
Kuchen	kookh'n	cake
Milch	milsh	milk
Mineralwasser	minn-er-arl-vuss-er	mineral water
Öl	erl	oil
Pfeffer	pfeff-er	pepper
Rindfleisch	rint-flysh	beef
Saft	zuft	juice
Salat	zal-aat	salad
Salz	zults	salt
Salzkartoffeln	zults-kar-toff'l	boiled potatoes
Sekt	zekt	sparkling wine
scharf	sharf	spicy
Schnitzel	shnitz'l	veal/pork cutlet
Schweinefleisch	shvine-flysh	pork
Spargel	shparg'l	asparagus
Spinat	shpin-art	spinach
Tee	tay	tea
Wein	vine	wine
Wiener Würstchen	veen-er voorst-sh'n	frankfurter
Zucker	tsook-er	sugar
Zwiebel	tsveeb'l	onion

Numbers

0	null	nool
1	eins	eye'ns
2	zwei	tsvy
3	drei	dry
4	vier	feer
5	fünf	foonf
6	sechs	zex
7	sieben	zeeb'n
8	acht	uhkht
9	neun	noyn
10	zehn	tsayn
11	elf	elf
12	zwölf	tserlf
13	dreizehn	dry-tsayn
14	vierzehn	feer-tsayn
15	fünfzehn	foonf-tsayn
16	sechzehn	zex-tsayn
17	siebzehn	zeep-tsayn
18	achtzehn	uhkht-tsayn
19	neunzehn	noyn-tsayn
20	zwanzig	tsvunn-tsig
21	einundzwanzig	ine-oont-tsvunn-tsig
30	dreissig	dry-sig
40	vierzig	feer-sig
50	fünfzig	foonf-tsig
60	sechzig	zex-tsig
70	siebzig	zeep-tsig
80	achtzig	uhkht-tsig
90	neunzig	noyn-tsig
100	hundert	hoond't
1000	tausend	towz'nt
1,000,000	eine Million	ine-uh mill-yon

Time

one minute	eine Minute	ine-uh min-oot-uh
one hour	eine Stunde	ine-uh shtoond-uh
Monday	Montag	mohn-targ
Tuesday	Dienstag	deens-targ
Wednesday	Mittwoch	mitt-vokh
Thursday	Donnerstag	donn-ers-targ
Friday	Freitag	fry-targ
Saturday	Samstag	zums-targ
Sunday	Sonntag	zon-targ